THE WORLD TO COME

THE

WORLD

TO COME

The Guides'
Long-Awaited Predictions
for the Dawning Age

BY

RUTH
MONTGOMERY

THREE RIVERS PRESS · NEW YORK

Published by Three Rivers Press, New York, New York.
Member of the Crown Publishing Group.

Random House, Inc. New York, Toronto, London, Sydney, Auckland
www.randomhouse.com

THREE RIVERS PRESS is a registered trademark and the Three Rivers Press colophon is a trademark of Random House, Inc.

Originally published in hardcover by Harmony Books in 1999.

Printed in the United States of America

DESIGN BY KAREN MINSTER

Library of Congress Cataloging-in-Publication Data

Montgomery, Ruth Shick, 1912–
      The world to come : the guides' long-awaited predictions for the dawning age
Montgomery. — 1st ed.
      1. Spirit writings.   2. Prophecies (Occultism).   3. Twenty-first
century—Forecasts—Miscellanea.   I. Title
BF1311.P75M66   1999
133.9'3—dc21   99-13083

ISBN 0-609-80537-1

10 9 8 7 6 5 4 3 2 1

FIRST PAPERBACK EDITION

To
MY DEAR FRIEND
LEIZE PERLMUTTER,
WHOSE HELP IS
INESTIMABLE

CONTENTS

THE WORLD TO COME

Many changes have occurred since the last time that my faithful readers and I have met between the covers of a new book. Previously I had been bringing forth a book with the Guides at approximately one-year intervals, but there are good reasons why I have allowed over a dozen years to elapse since the last one, as I shall herein explain.

As many of you are aware, I was a syndicated Washington columnist writing on politics and world affairs at the time that I had my first encounters with the psychic world, in the 1960s. Twenty years earlier I had begun my Washington career by covering the White House press conferences of President Franklin D. Roosevelt, and I was the last president of Mrs. Roosevelt's White House press conferences, dissolving the organization at the time of the president's death. I had also been elected president of the Women's National Press Club (now merged with the National Press Club) and during the ensuing years had covered every national nominating convention and traveled with the presidential candidates on their campaigns. I had also traveled abroad to interview heads of states, and covered the State Department and Congress in their Washington activities.

Like most newspaper reporters, I had little awareness of psychic happenings, and no belief in them whatsoever. Then my sister-in-law, Rhoda Montgomery, insisted that my husband and I accompany her to a séance in St. Petersburg, Florida, and we reluctantly agreed. So many intriguing messages came through that I could not explain that I told my editor about it, and Kingsbury Smith, the president of International News Service (INS), asked me to write a series of articles on what happens to a female reporter who goes to séances. This sounded like a refreshing change of pace from going to the White House and Congress every day in pursuit of news, so I went to many darkened-room séances and apparently communicated with ghosts instead of politicians and diplomats.

My ensuing eight-part series ran in hundreds of newspapers throughout the country, and to our amazement it produced more response from readers than anything else that INS had ever published. As a doubter myself, I had not tried to sell the subject, and I carefully pointed out the incidences that to me seemed fraudulent, as well as those for which I could find no other explanation than otherworldly. Later I incorporated some of the material into a book called *A Search for the Truth*.

By that time I had met Arthur Ford, the noted medium who broke the Houdini code that the famous magician and his wife had created before his death, to see if whichever one passed on first could actually contact the other. While in a deep trance Ford succeeded in making contact with Houdini, and conveyed his spirit message to his wife through the code. Intrigued by this, I attended a speech that Ford delivered at a church in Washington, D.C., and afterward asked if I might interview him for my column. He acquiesced, offered a séance, and during it brought in my deceased father, who gave me evidential information that Ford himself could not have known. We became friends, and Ford subsequently declared he was receiving psychically that I would be able to do automatic writing. He explained that this meant receiving material written on paper from entities who were now in the spirit plane, and told me how to proceed.

Always keen for a new adventure, but exceedingly skeptical, I sat daily at the same hour at my desk and, after meditation and a silent prayer for protection, rested a pencil tip lightly on a sheet of paper. For days nothing happened, but on the tenth day the pencil began to write, and when later I opened my eyes I could read messages from deceased family members. Then one day it drew a lily, wrote the word *Lily* with a flourish, and announced that thereafter he would identify himself in that manner. Beautiful philosophy began to flow from the daily writing, and since then Lily has gathered together a group of discarnates who have dictated most of the material for my fifteen books. After his death Arthur Ford joined the writing group, and I now refer to them collectively as the Guides.

One morning I overslept, and noting that it was time for my daily session with the Guides, I reached for a pencil and pad and sat on the side of the bed while the writing began. But suddenly it was as if a giant hand had been placed over mine; it wrote so heavily and emphatically that I opened my eyes and read: "WE SAID GO TO YOUR TYPEWRITER."

I then read the previous writing, which had explained that it was getting difficult to read the scrawl, because it was coming so fast, and that they felt they had now developed the power to type through me. I dutifully crossed the hall to my home office, sat at my typewriter, flicked on the power, and placed my fingers in touch-typing position. The clicking of the keys told me that writing was coming through, and from then on the messages flowed much more rapidly. And so it continued.

Upon completing *A Search for the Truth,* Lily announced that we would now do a book on reincarnation. I protested that I didn't even believe in it, but he calmly wrote that this was no problem. "Just research it like you did the psychic field," he commented, "and we will give you proof." I did so, and the resultant book was *Here and Hereafter.* This was when Arthur Ford died, and after joining the group he dictated fascinating material about continuing life in the spirit plane. That led to *A World Beyond,* and readers showered me with letters saying that it was the most comforting book they had ever read, removing all fear of death.

It was also quite influential, because it apparently gave prominent doctors the courage to write about the near-death experiences that some of their patients had recounted to them, in which they too described life in the spirit plane. The Guides declared that at death we do not go to a different sphere, but simply change our own vibrations. Those who have died are here, but we don't see them. An example is an electric fan; when it is turned on, we see the individual blades easily, but as the vibration speeds up we see through them.

In my next books *The World Before, Strangers Among Us,* and *Threshold to Tomorrow,* the Guides wrote about how the world began, and about Walk-ins, who, having advanced sufficiently in previous lifetimes, can return to the bodies of adults (instead of babies), exchanging places with souls who desperately want to depart, or who through illness or accidents cannot maintain the spark of life. But then they began to write about a shift of the Earth on its axis near the turn of this century, to which the famed seers Nostradamus and Edgar Cayce had also referred. This frightened some of my readers, who could not face the thought of so-called death and wanted to know how they could save themselves and their families. Some even panicked and moved to areas that they considered safer.

After Arthur Ford died and joined the group, we have written a number of books together. In them the Guides have made innumerable predictions, nearly all of which have already come to pass. Some of them have been specific, foretelling the outcome of presidential elections, the ousting of foreign leaders, and the adverse weather conditions that we are currently undergoing: flooding, earthquakes, drought, and famine. They have also foreseen the outcome of problems besetting some of my inquiring friends, and given me personal advice that proved unerringly correct.

Like every other reasonably intelligent human being, I sometimes experience doubt, wondering if my own subconscious could be producing such results. Each time, however, I encounter still another proof that I could not conceivably have known about a situation or correctly guessed the outcome.

Within the past year my personal physician, who is aware of my psychic interest, asked during a routine office visit whether I had ever heard of a man whom I shall call Marshall Brown. I replied in the negative, and he remarked that I might ask the Guides about him. I agreed to do so if he would write down the name for me, and I have before me Dr. Joseph Spano's prescription sheet on which he wrote: "Is there anything that I should know about Marshall Brown, M.D.?"

Now I was uncomfortable. Here was one physician asking me about another physician, with no information supplied except that the latter did not live in Naples, Florida, where I do. I felt that my Guides were being tested, and it made me nervous. Nevertheless, at the next day's session I typed out Dr. Spano's question, and after my meditation the Guides wrote: "Tell Joe Spano that the other doctor has a rare malignancy that is difficult to pinpoint as to the proper treatment. As you know, we are not doctors, but that very good man needs skilled attention in diagnosis and fine-tuning. Joe Spano is a very old soul who can reach within and intuit well, and be extremely helpful to any specialists who are called into the case."

After the session I typed out a copy of the writing for Dr. Spano and then nearly lost my nerve. What if there was nothing wrong with Dr. Brown? What if my own doctor was merely checking on the other's character? After all, his question hinted at no physical disability.

Taking courage in hand, I dropped off the copy at my doctor's office . . . and then heard nothing from him. Well, if I had disgraced myself, I could always change doctors, although I did not relish the thought. A couple of months later, when I was again in Dr. Spano's office for a scheduled appointment, I made no mention of the previous incident. As I was leaving, the busy doctor said, "Oh, by the way, that information you brought me was right on the nose. It's precisely correct."

My relief was short-lived. Dr. Spano called me back to say that a friend of his had lost his father four or five months previously and wondered why he had not been contacted from the other side. Again he gave me only his name, which was totally unfamiliar to me. Cheered by our recent success, I asked the Guides about Scott Wiesen, and the Guides produced the deceased father, who gave his son detailed instructions on how to make direct contact with him through daily meditation at the same hour. He also described his life in the spirit plane and sent his love.

At the next day's session I asked if the Guides had anything to add to the message for Scott, and they wrote: "As to Marvin [the father], he wants Scott to remember a time when the two of them were talking philosophically about death, and Scott said he would like to have proof of an afterlife. Tell him he has it now, and will be able to convince himself through his own communication, if he will follow the advice Marvin gave him yesterday through your Guides."

I dutifully typed out the messages and again dropped them off at my doctor's office. Three days later I received a telephone call from a young woman in Massachusetts whose words came tumbling out in her excitement. "Forgive me for bothering you," she began, "but I'm Scott Wiesen's sister, and we're all terribly excited about your messages from my father. Everything sounds exactly like him, and we have no doubt at all that those communications come from him."

She chatted on for some time about how happy her mother and other family members were to receive the news and then remarked that her brother was a doctor who often worked with Dr. Spano. Another doctor! I finally broke in to ask, "Did Scott ever have the alleged discussion to which your father referred?"

"Oh, yes!" she exclaimed. "My father not only had that discussion with Scott, but he had the identical talk with me before he died. It's all true!"

Shortly thereafter Scott's mother flew down to visit her son, and telephoned to add her verification to the messages. Then I met the young doctor in person, and after he had thanked me for contacting his father, I asked if he was following the instructions to make his own personal contact. He replied rather lamely that he had been "just too busy to try" the meditation and automatic writing.

Because the Guides seem to activate only my typing fingers and not my mind in conveying their information, I do not remember what they write, and it would be lost unless the words were recorded on paper. After I deliver a message to a specific individual who has requested information, it also seems to be erased from my memory bank.

This explains another incident that is seemingly evidential. Recently I went to a lecture at Unity Church, and was glad to be joined by former U.S. Congressman Berkley Bedell and his wife, Elinor, who spotted me as they entered and took two vacant seats directly behind me.

Before the speaker took over the podium, Berkley leaned forward and remarked, "Ruth, your Guides were certainly right about my heart." I looked at him blankly. I had not seen the Bedells for several months and had no recollection of any such previous conversation.

"Don't you remember that when I thought I was having heart problems, your Guides said that I did not?" he prompted. "Since then I've wasted several thousand dollars having every kind of test, and the doctors agree that my heart is fine."

On returning home, I shuffled through the drawer where I keep the automatic writing. In a message dated January 8, 1994, which actually concerned the Bedells' daughter, the Guides had added: "Berkley Bedell is needlessly worried about his heart. It seems okay from our vantage point." I had obviously included that sentence when mailing them the message for their daughter.

In recent years the Guides have continued to talk about the impending Shift, but since I did not wish to write another alarming book, I desisted. Now, however, the Guides assert that the Shift will be postponed at least until 2010 or 2012, because they say that they have long foreseen an American Walk-in president firmly installed in office before the Shift, with the ability to assist Earthlings during that trying time. The Guides stress that although the timing is in God's hands and man cannot alter God's will, "it is possible that so many enlightened beings have now entered the Earth and helped to lift the consciousness that it is not necessary for so much destruction."

As examples, they pointed to the thousands of enlightened Walk-ins who have returned to adult bodies, and also to many survivors of the Hundred Years' War in Europe who are now reincarnated and are determined to prevent more bloodshed in needless wars.

Another good influence, apparently, is the present reincarnation of several of the Apostles and other Palestinians from biblical times who were devoted followers of Jesus Christ. The Guides identified some of these to me, and this seemed to provide exciting new material for a book. Also, my beloved husband, Bob, passed on several years ago and has now joined a growing number of discarnates and my readers in pleading for another book. We will go into greater detail about all of these events as we proceed with this book about the world to come.

THE WORLD TO COME

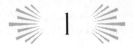

1

MESSAGES FROM BEYOND

My daily communication with the Guides continued for many years, though Lily steadfastly refused to identify himself until they began dictating material for *Companions Along the Way,* a book about ten of my previous lives in which I had known Arthur Ford. At last Lily declared that in one of his incarnations he had been Savonarola, the martyred Italian Dominican priest who was burned on a cross in fifteenth-century Florence for refusing to retract his fiery writings against the corruption of the Catholic Church and the de Medici court. At that point I could not have identified Savonarola if asked, but the Guides wrote of him: "He was mystical; a sensitive who was aware of others' intentions and secret thoughts, but he was practical in his application of the laws of God to man, desiring freedom and equality for all men and eager to direct them inward to the search for God rather than outward to the search for personal gain. Some considered him a fanatic, and perhaps he was, in his burning zeal to reform state and humankind, but so powerful was his message and his performance that he influenced the course of history and rang a bell for liberty that is still to be heard. A godly man who gave his life for those ideals that knew no boundaries of nation or creed."

The *Encyclopaedia Britannica,* I soon discovered, was equally laudatory about Savonarola. In a 1950s volume it recounts that he was "born to an excellent family in 1452, scorned court life and entered a Dominican order, where he wrote poems of burning indignation against the corruption of Church and court. A mystic, he had prophetic visions that came true, and he seemed to read others' minds." It further states that for a time he even became the lawgiver for Florence, "relieving the suffering of the starving and reducing taxes on the lower classes. He guarded the public weal with extraordinary wisdom" and almost overnight changed pleasure-loving Florence into an ascetic regime. "Because he assailed the corruption of the Vatican and Pope Alexander VI, the Borgia who bought the papal throne, he was excommunicated and after forty days of torture was given a mock trial. But he refused to recant his charges and bravely submitted to burning on a cross.

He left behind an immense number of devotional and moral essays, numerous sermons, some poems, and a political treatise on the government of Florence." I was astonished to learn that everything the Guides had written about this notable figure was thus verified.

The Guides contributed that Arthur Ford was then an intimate counselor and assistant to Savonarola, "who threw in his lot with this man who had the power to lift humankind out of itself to higher planes of wisdom." They said Ford was then known as Father Gabrielli and that I did not know them then because I was not incarnate during that horrendous period. But the Guides, in *Companions Along the Way,* related other lifetimes when both Lily and Ford were my father, which could explain why they have been willing to put up with me and communicate through all of these decades. They also recounted numerous lifetimes when my husband, Bob, and I were said to have been husband and wife.

The Guides and I continued to collaborate on books until, after publication of my fifteenth one, Bob declared in exasperation: "If you write another book, I'm leaving." I knew the threat was an idle one, but subconsciously it influenced me. Perhaps I *should* be paying more attention to my husband instead of spreading the teachings of unseen Guides to unknown readers. I seemed unable to start another book. I continued to correspond occasionally with the Guides, but I lacked the inspiration to disseminate it.

We moved from Washington, D.C., to Naples, Florida, and life sailed smoothly along until Bob's health began to fail. On a Sunday night, January 31, 1993, I had just slipped into bed when the telephone rang. Lifting the receiver, I listened in stunned silence as a female voice began, "Mrs. Montgomery, I'm sorry to tell you that your husband is gone."

"Gone!" I finally found the voice to say.

"Yes," the nurse at the nursing home where Bob was a new resident continued, "I checked on him only a short time ago and he seemed all right, but when I went in just now I found him dead. We're not permitted to keep a body here overnight. What arrangements do you want to make?" Thus ended my fifty-seven years of marriage to Bob Montgomery . . . or so it seemed.

Strange how the mental processes continue to function almost automatically while the emotional system goes into numbed shock. I called my sister, Margaret Forry, in Indianapolis, and she said she would be on the first available flight. Then I dialed my second cousin, Phil Cunningham, who spends the winter season at a nearby villa, and that wonderful man said he would go immediately to the nursing home and oversee the removal of Bob's body to Hodges Funeral Home. The next morning I went with Phil to identify the remains and supply information for Bob's obituary. Margaret arrived later that day, and after Bob's body was cremated, we held a memorial service with close friends on Friday.

Meanwhile, I had managed to perform all the perfunctory tasks: notifying our lawyer, the bank, and Bob's relatives, and meeting with our good friend Ninette Peterson, an ordained minister whom Bob and I had previously chosen to conduct our services if she were available when our time came.

Outwardly I was functioning normally. Inwardly I felt like a robot who had been put on automatic pilot. I couldn't cry. I couldn't grieve. As a matter of fact, I dared not grieve, because I was acutely aware of my Guides' warning about that many years before, while writing *A Search for the Truth.* In a chapter of that book, entitled "The Selfishness of Grief," the Guides detailed how overly grieving survivors keep a loved one Earthbound and thereby retard the spiritual progress of a soul newly crossed into the spirit plane. Bob was the best person I have ever known. He deserved better than a grieving widow who was feeling sorry for herself and moaning about her loss.

I was confident that Bob was still alive, although in an altered state of consciousness. I also knew that he could not have been strong and healthy again in physical being. A year before his so-called death, he had suddenly hemorrhaged in the middle of the night, and by the time an ambulance arrived he had lost a third of his blood supply. His doctor chose not to give him transfusions, for fear that the local blood supply was contaminated, and he was thus unable to regain the weight that he had lost. Nor the energy!

The hemorrhaging was unrelated to an aneurysm of his aorta that had existed for several years. Before long, his doctor was insisting that he have an operation to correct the problem, and although I protested that Bob was not yet strong enough to withstand such intrusive surgery, Bob finally agreed to it.

From then on, for the next five months, he was in and out of hospitals and nursing homes repeatedly. I would bring him home again and again, where he wanted to be, but then find myself dialing 911 to rush him back to the hospital for heart failure or a fall. He returned to a nursing home only three days before the call came that he was "gone." I had spent several hours that Sunday with him, pushing his wheelchair out to a lake on the grounds to watch the ducks waddle around. Then I wheeled him inside to a newer section of the facility where a larger, brighter room had just become available. He was to be moved there the following morning, and he seemed happy about the arrangements. His demise, when it came, was therefore a shock to all of us.

During the traumatic months of Bob's illness, I had been too physically and emotionally drained to continue my sessions with the Guides. Surely, I thought, I would be forgiven by those sometimes stern taskmasters for using what little strength I had to work for Bob's recovery. Finally, twelve days after his passing, I returned to my typewriter and timorously asked the Guides, "Is Bob aware yet, and is there anything you can tell me about him, please?"

I then meditated, silently prayed for protection, and placed my fingers in touch-typing position, whereupon they sprang to action, writing: "Bob is wide awake and laughing at your query about whether he is aware. He has received all your thoughts about him and knows how much you love him. He says, 'Ruth, honey, don't worry about a thing. You were wonderful, simply wonderful, throughout that long ordeal, and I love you with my whole heart. I've seen Rhoda and Burke [Bob's sister and brother], Mother and Father and all of the others, and it's wonderful to be free and without pain again. Bertha and Ira [my parents] are with us, and we're having a real reunion. Listen, honey, it's just like you described it in your books, and there is nothing for you to worry about. Everything will work out there, and you'll get a lot of help from this side, just as you have been getting it all these years. Please forgive me, and I know you do, for all that I've put you through these last few months. Didn't think my body would wear out so soon, but it's just a body, and we'll be together again, make no mistake about that.'" The Guides then signed off, saying that they would be in touch with me shortly.

I resumed my sessions with the Guides, but only sporadically, as I was swamped with the details of settling up our joint estate, making a new will, answering mail and telephone calls from sympathetic friends, and trying to put our affairs in order. I invariably date my communications with the Guides, and I note that three months elapsed before I again typed out a query about Bob: "Tell me more about him now, please."

After my meditation, the writing began: "Bob is here and says, 'Honey, I love you and am so sorry to have worn you down these last months. Forgive me, please. As for my work now, I have been reviewing that life and see some real errors that I made, but most of them were unintentional. I tried to be what I thought was a good man, and I hope I succeeded to some extent. Well, we had a good life together, didn't we, and I'm proud of you. Just keep trying hard to be calm and serene, and do by all means go out with friends. Don't become too attached to staying at home, as I'm afraid I did those last few years. It isn't a very healthy attitude. Here I'm seeing relatives and friends, including [here he mentioned some by name] from my earlier days. Also, many of our mutual friends in later years.'" Then he signed off with loving words.

Bob's ashes were in an engraved urn that I had brought home with me after the memorial service. We had both decided on cremation several years previously, and our head-stone was already erected in a family plot at the cemetery in Sumner, Illinois, where my parents, grandparents, and even a great-great-grandfather are buried.

That spring Sigma Delta Chi, the professional journalism society, notified me that I was to be inducted into the Journalism Hall of Fame and invited me to DePauw University for the ceremony. I not only appreciated the honor but regarded it as a splendid opportunity to arrange the burial of Bob's ashes during the same trip, since Sumner was not too far from Greencastle, Indiana, and my sister, Margaret, would be with me there. Other relatives could meet us in Sumner, where I was born.

A couple of weeks before my departure I was seated in the den in my usual chair facing the television set, with Bob's matching chair separated from mine only by an end table and lamp, when internally I suddenly heard his voice repeating the words that he had spoken there once, but which I had completely forgotten. Even the plaintive tone was identical, saying: "Ruth, I don't know that I want to be up there in the cemetery all alone until you come."

Of course! How could I not have remembered? After all, those were *my* ancestors, not *his,* and although I felt completely at home there, because I had been visiting the graves of my ancestors since earliest childhood, he did not share those memories. Needless to say, the urn with Bob's ashes continues to occupy the place of honor in an antique glass cabinet in the foyer of our house.

On my birthday in June I asked the Guides: "Is Bob glad that I keep his ashes here?" Lily (my principal guide) came through first, and then brought in Bob, who wrote: "Happy birthday, sweetheart. Yes, I'm so very pleased that you want to keep them there with you." He then continued with loving sentiments.

Three months later I mustered enough courage to begin a session with this question to the Guides: "Would Bob rather be in spirit or in flesh? What is he doing with his time? What is it like there—or is it here, not there?" The latter was a reference to a comment made by Lily many years before that "we're not up there, or out there somewhere, we're here."

Bob's reply to my question may interest other widows. "Honey," he wrote, "I'd rather be with you in flesh, but this is the next best alternative. We are rarely troubled by things on the earthly plane, since we see a wider spectrum, but we do care about those still there and wish we could help more. We keep busy here with a variety of interests: the schools that Arthur Ford told you about in *A World Beyond* and the various so-called temples where we try to shed faults and improve our spiritual selves. It's hard to describe to one in your plane, but we are there and here and anywhere that we choose to be at a given flicker of time. In fact, we're not aware of time, except for schedules that we set for ourselves, as the Guides have done with your automatic writing sessions. Do keep them up, Ruth, as we would like to see one more book about what is to come. Yes, I know I discouraged you then, but now I understand much better." That was indeed a change of attitude!

On the first anniversary of Bob's passing, I prefaced my meditation by writing: "It is a year since Bob went into spirit. I'd like for him to tell me what his passing over was like, and how he has found it in the spirit plane. If he's not prepared to do so today, perhaps soon."

"Here's Bob," the Guides promptly declared, and he wrote: "Hi, honey. The passing over, as you term it, was easy as pie. I felt a choking sensation and some coughing as my lungs filled up with fluid; then a great peace as the choking stopped. There was a light ahead, and I simply followed it, and all at once I glimpsed Rhoda and Burke and some other family members, including Bertha, Ira, and Paul [my brother], and I could recognize them all, even though they seemed light in comparison with what I termed their normal builds. They were all very welcoming, but as I looked back, the nurse was telephoning you, and I felt such closeness to you, and regret at your sorrow. But you did all the right things, honey, calling Marg and

Philip, and they were so good to take care of details. I liked the short memorial service, and Ninette did a great job, just as we had hoped she would when our time came.

"Since then I've been studying some, as Arthur said we would, and also reviewing my past life, often with some regrets, but also with a feeling of satisfaction that I did not yield to temptations and overstep the bounds of decorum. I tried to live up to my father, always, as you know [Bob's father was a Methodist minister who died before I met Bob], and it was wonderful to see him here again, as well as Mother and others. In a way, I feel like we're marking time here. No big hurdles or decisions to make, and of course we're all aware of the changes that are coming to planet Earth. Lily says there will be a mighty avalanche of souls arriving all at once when the Shift occurs, and that we should be ready to ease their passage. There's a lot I have to learn between now and then, and I'll do my best to be helpful. I love you, Bob."

Besides a bill for final services, I had heard nothing from Bob's doctor after his passing, although we had both been under his care for seven years. Nor did I hear again from anyone at the nursing home. Bob had been alone at the time, so there was no one to ask about his final minutes. I was sent a copy of the death certificate, which listed "ventricular fibrillation" as the cause of death, but that told me nothing about the so-called death throes.

At last, seventeen months later, I asked the Guides if Bob could give me a more detailed account of his physical death and passage into spirit. The Guides produced Bob for me, and he wrote: "Hi, honey. Well, it wasn't pleasant in those last few minutes. I seemed to be choking and gasping for breath, and I rang for the nurse, but she didn't come. The next thing, I blacked out. Then I saw a light ahead and thought maybe I was being wheeled down the corridor to the emergency room, but it was the tunnel that people talk about. As the light became brighter I could see brilliant colors and hear music. Then let's see. I think I saw Burke and Rhoda first, and then a whole bunch of family members, including my Grandma Montgomery [who died when he was a boy]. It was then I realized that I had left the body behind and was starting a new adventure, as you would have called it. At first it was very exciting, but then I looked back at you and felt very sad that we weren't together and wondered how you would get along alone. Ira and Bertha came and said you had a lot of grit and would make it just fine, and suddenly I knew they were right.

"Since then I see some of them fairly regularly, though we are into a training program, I guess you'd call it, assessing ourselves and looking ahead to what we want to accomplish in our development. I don't miss that body at all, though it served in good stead for a nice long time, until it began to collapse on me. This is a beautiful place, and all wants are met with love and kindness; but I do miss you, honey, though I'm with you a lot more than you realize. Take care of yourself and know that I love you."

Perusing this lengthy message after the writing ceased, I was fascinated by one of Bob's comments. In describing his death experience, he said he had thought he was being wheeled down the corridor toward a bright light, "but it was the tunnel that people talk about."

That was a stunner, coming from Bob! Those of us who are interested in the psychic field are familiar with recent books about near-death experiences, in which the revived patient tells of going through a tunnel toward a light. But Bob had never read books in the psychic field, and I had never written about the tunnels or discussed them with Bob. The only explanation that seems logical is that he and others have exchanged experiences since all of them are in the spirit plane. This would seem to validate the near-death experiences reported by those who have survived in physical being.

Another of my birthdays rolled around, and after a nice greeting from the Guides, Bob wrote: "Honey, I wish I were there to celebrate with you. Growing old in physical being is not much fun, but the Guides want you to stay well and round out your lifespan with one more book. I love you. Here's Bertha."

My mother, who had so opposed my writing books in the psychic field while she was here, came in, saying: "Ruthie, I take back all I said about your beliefs, because you were right. It's not what we expected to find over here, by any means, but it's interesting, and we're all continuing to strive toward the right thing, and to help others in any way that we can. We're proud of you and love you. Here's Ira."

My dad came through, writing: "Hi, kiddo. Yes, that about wraps it up. It's a continuation here of what we all tried to do there: be good and kind and helpful, as we are all striving for spiritual advancement. There are not the temptations here that we had there: to make more money or get ahead of the other fellow. Spread the word and be a good girl. Much love, Dad."

It was nice to have that family visit, and I am sure that it will be pleasant to see all the good friends and relatives who have preceded us into spirit, but it all began to sound rather boring. Certainly it seemed to lack the fun and excitement of my college days and my long newspaper career in Washington. After all, here on the earthly plane we also have friends and relatives, whom we can physically hug.

As usual, I had my comeuppance. The very next day Bob tried to set the record straight, writing: "It is not true that we have no bodies here, for the spirit body is just as real to us here as the physical one was there, except that this one gives us no problems and seems to need no attention. We're just *here,* and we know each other just as we did while there. It isn't boring at all! It's quite stimulating, and there's so much to learn that we don't like to idle away time. Nearly everyone seems busy at something or other, and although I have a lot to learn, it's interesting to assimilate these new ideas from various sources, review our past life for errors, and formulate what we want to accomplish from here on out."

Bob had mentioned "past life" in the singular, and since the Guides have told me of other lives that I shared with Bob, as well as with them *(Companions Along the Way),* I asked in the next session whether Bob had looked into any previous lifetimes.

He replied: "I haven't done much work yet with those lives, although I am aware that there have been plenty of them. Here's Lily." My principal Guide then took over, writing: "Ruth, that comes later, after the assessment of the immediate past life is pretty well completed. Bob is getting along fine, at his own pace."

After completing *Companions Along the Way,* the Guides had discussed the beginnings of humankind on planet Earth, and the lost continents of Lemuria and Atlantis. They further foretold a shift of the Earth on its axis at the close of this century, an event that they said had occurred several times before the beginning of our recorded history. The findings of numerous geologists and scientists seemed to confirm their assertions, and so I wrote *The World Before.*

Surely, I thought afterward, there was nothing more to say about the psychic realm, and I prepared to relax. But the Guides had a different scenario for me. They apparently arranged for a young woman to write me a letter that began: "I wish that you would write a book about Walk-ins."

What in the world were Walk-ins? When I wrote back to ask her, she responded, "Ask your Guides." Properly rebuked, I did so, and the information that poured through my automatic typewriting eventually produced two books: *Strangers Among Us* and *Threshold to Tomorrow.* The resultant fan mail was overwhelming. So many wrote to describe their own near-death experiences and their total change of personality and attitude afterward, while begging me to ask the Guides if they were Walk-ins, that I had to prepare a form letter regretting that the Guides could no longer identify Walk-ins. There simply wasn't time to ask them about thousands of individual cases, and the Guides said that this was not their mission.

Many of my readers wrote to ask about reports of UFO sightings that were rampant in the news. I queried the Guides, and they began to divulge a vast quantity of material about extraterrestrial beings who were visiting our planet, contacting individuals, or entering earthly bodies through the Walk-in process. This led to *Aliens Among Us.*

Thereafter the Guides seemed determined to return to the theme of preparing for the Shift and the immediate period thereafter. Each time I exclaimed that I did not want to write another scary book about the Shift. Surely we had covered that sufficiently in our previous books.

The Guides have never learned to take no for an answer. They persisted, and so did my fan mail, in talking about the Shift. At last, in desperation, I prefaced a session by writing: "I don't want to write a book that worries people. If we do write another manuscript together, I'd like it to stress that there's nothing to fear. You have taught me that we go on living, whether in flesh or spirit, and that there's no such thing as death. What do you think of that idea?"

Following my meditation, they wrote: "That is the theme we would like to take. Those who feel discouraged or frightened by the thought of the Shift should realize that *they* go on, whether in or out of the physical body. The essence is in the spirit—the soul. Bodies gradually wear out, or get pushed about and destroyed, but that has nothing to do with the essence, the *you.* We are all eternal. Having been created as sparks of the Creator at the beginning of time, we do not perish. The good lives on, and as for the bad, we return again and again to physical form in order to recompense for our errors and learn needed lessons. The true life is of the spirit, not the flesh. Why some wish to cling forever to their physical bodies is beyond reason in our sphere, for as we pay back karma and develop new insights we gradually eliminate the need to return to physical form. Life is in the spirit, not the body."

2

DELAY OF THE SHIFT

Some of the faithful readers of my books have understandingly become a little irritated with me in recent years. Why, they want to know, have I not continued to report on the messages from my Guides? A few have written that I "owe it" to them to disclose what the Guides are divulging about the impending shift of the Earth on its axis. After all, they had predicted that event to occur around the end of this decade, and we are rapidly approaching the deadline. What is going on?

They are not alone in their complaints. The Guides were so insistent on my writing "one last book" that I finally asked them what the main focus of this joint effort should be. I was willing to oblige, but only if they would disclose startling new revelations that could assist us all.

They began that day's discourse with these words: "Why not focus on the changing patterns of thought: things accepted now almost as a matter of fact, like reincarnation, alien sightings, psychic phenomena, meditation, and communication between the living and so-called dead that were virtually unheard of by the majority of Americans when you first began your investigation of the field thirty-some years ago? Nowadays these subjects blanket television and radio, newspapers and magazines, seminars and symposiums, and books galore written by doctors, psychiatrists, psychologists, and psychics. Everything is speeding up because of the imminence of the shift of the Earth on its axis, and the need for Earthlings to understand and prepare for such a stupendous event. People are beginning to realize the importance of preparing one's soul for passage into spirit and the continuing life beyond, or, for those who wish to remain in flesh, to acquire seeds, staples, tools, safe housing, and the like. Time is of the essence."

Judging by my fan mail, many are disturbed about the predictions made by my Guides, famed psychic Edgar Cayce, Nostradamus, and others of an impending shift around the turn of the century. They want to know if their present areas will be safe or where they should go. I do not like to be an alarmist. I dislike writing about gloomy subjects, and I have therefore stalled for a number of years, despite the pleas of my readers to tell them what the Guides are foreseeing in the future.

I explained this problem to the Guides, who wrote: "When a person faces an uncertain future, it is best for him to view it as an opportunity for personal growth and not to be fearful of the unknown." This led us to a discussion of the present with the forecasts of chaotic alterations.

Referring to the predicted Shift, they continued: "We see here that it is inescapable for those on Earth. Therefore it should in no way be feared, for life goes on, and it is the attitude of the soul that matters most, before, during, and after the transition into spirit. Those who survive in body will find the knowledge deep within them and know how to cope with the unleashed forces of nature. They should have no worries, for the Shift itself is rapid and the Earth quickly stabilizes in its new position relative to the sun and moon. Busy hands will replace idle chatter, and they will joyously take charge of the altered methods of survival. Those who pass into spirit will awaken to dramatic changes as well. So many will make the passage at once that few loved ones will seem to be lost to them, and joyous will be the reunions in this spirit stage of constant living. The importance lies in letting go of fears and the repining for lost possessions, instead accepting the benevolence of a Creator who made it possible for them to find other loved ones and to unravel so many puzzles of life."

Continuing, they wrote: "They will be greeted here by parents, grandparents, and many others who are awaiting their arrival, and at the same time they will not be truly separated from those still in fleshly garb. Their minds will be opened, and before long, direct communication with them will be possible, as they learn new tools for communication between the various spheres of eternal life."

This latter is an apparent reference to the Guides' assertion in previous books that in the millennium that is to be ushered in by the Shift, Earthly inhabitants will be able to communicate through extrasensory perception, not only with one another but also with many of those in the spirit realm.

Approximately five years ago the Guides said that they now foresaw a delay in the Shift, explaining: "We have always told you that we could not tell you its exact time, because that is in God's hands. But we have also foreseen a Walk-in American president in place before then, preparing jobs and housing in safe areas. Since we do not now see a Walk-in president during this last decade of the century, we feel certain that the Shift will be delayed."

Inasmuch as no Walk-in candidate is yet in sight, this would indicate that no shift will occur before 2010 or 2012, since four years elapse between our presidential elections, and the then-president would require a few years to put his plan into operation after his election. In recent years I have thus been sending this information to those readers of my books who wrote to ask me about the Shift.

So to those worried ones who had been preparing to tear up their current lifestyles and move to places that they reasoned would provide safer abodes, the message seemed to be: "Unpack and relax."

Readers of my previous books are aware of the Guides' prediction that a Walk-in will become president of the United States before the Shift occurs, and will be extremely helpful in preparing our nation, as well as others, with sage advice.

For those unfamiliar with the term, the Guides define Walk-ins as high-minded entities from the spirit plane who are permitted under certain circumstances to take over the unwanted bodies of other human beings, who then depart into spirit. The motivation for the Walk-ins must be humanitarian, to help others and benefit humankind. The exchange cannot be made for selfish purposes, and it bears no resemblance to the many documented cases of possession, in which multiple egos or malevolent spirits invade an inhabited body, creating havoc for all concerned.

The Walk-out must be one who desperately wishes to depart, or who because of a clinical death or near-death experience is unable to keep that body alive. The Walk-in, coming directly from the spirit plane, is able to reenergize the failing body; because of high idealism and enthusiasm, the personality of the new occupant often astounds friends and family members who have become accustomed to the discouraged or disinterested manner of the body's original occupant.

"Walk-ins are by no means perfected souls," the Guides cautioned. "They have faults like all the rest of us do, but because of their highly developed awareness, earned through previous lifetimes, they can receive permission to replace a soul in distress. By skipping babyhood and childhood, they can therefore get immediately to work on their new tasks."

Immediately following the 1992 elections, I received a number of letters asking if the newly elected president, Bill Clinton, was the Walk-in whom the Guides had predicted for the last decade of the twentieth century. On my asking the Guides, they wrote: "No, Clinton is not a Walk-in."

The Guides have consistently refused to make known the identity of the Walk-in president. They indicated that the transferal of egos occurred rather recently and that the current occupant of that body is not yet fully aware of his destiny, "although he has been through a traumatic experience that will awaken him to that awareness."

Referring to the worsening weather conditions throughout the globe that they predicted for the remainder of the decade, the Guides wrote: "People will be scurrying for cover as storms increase in velocity, and as famine in various parts of the underdeveloped world worsens, America will be unable to fill the needs because of its own economic conditions. The troubling times will make the office of the American presidency far less attractive to the able men and women who might otherwise be seeking it, and the Walk-in we have told you about will step forward."

Charles Dickens could have been foreseeing the last decade of the twentieth century when, in 1859, he began *A Tale of Two Cities* with these immortal lines:

> *It was the best of times, it was the worst of times, it was the age of wisdom, it was the age of foolishness, it was the epoch of belief, it was the epoch of incredulity, it was the season of Light, it was the season of Darkness, it was the spring of hope, it was the winter of despair.*

Who could describe today's world more aptly? We have an information superhighway that promises to bring us all knowledge and instant communication with virtually every person throughout the globe. Television already permits us to lounge in our homes while instantaneously viewing regional wars or sporting events on every continent, plus starving multitudes without homes or hope. Our newspapers bring us accounts of remarkable advances in the field of medicine or electronics, and also the latest details of gory murders or drug busts.

Radio and TV talk shows give everyday citizens ten seconds of fame as they express their opinions on everything from rape to matricide, condemning or condoning premeditated murder because the perpetrator had an "unhappy childhood," or disclosing their own bedroom secrets.

Religious zealots are damning all who disagree with their particular precepts, and warring factions in Eastern Europe, the Holy Land, Northern Ireland, and elsewhere are slaying one another in the name of religion.

Until recent years I had visualized the spirit plane as an idyllic Eden where everyone was peaceable and strove to do God's will. Nowadays, however, newspapers and television talk shows seem to have little to report but violent crimes, even by teenagers: murders, rapes, racial uprisings, and so-called ethnic cleansings that lead to the extermination of entire races and tribal units. Why, I asked the Guides, is there so much more violence now, and what will it be like in the spirit plane when so many souls who have committed such vicious acts arrive there simultaneously during the Shift?

They chose to respond to that double question in two parts,

first writing: "The youthful criminals today are the last gener-
ation of Atlanteans who will be entering the Earth in physical
form for a long time. Those of vicious nature are the violent
Atlanteans who helped to destroy their idyllic continent millennia ago. It's almost as if they feel time speeded up and want
to get in all of their evil deeds quickly, before time runs out for
them. These young people are, after all, old souls, not innocent
babes, and incarcerating them is about the best that can be
done in these remaining years before the Shift. Not many of
them will survive in flesh when the Shift occurs, and those who
do will perish before long.

"Their days are numbered on Earth, and on this side they are
condemning themselves to isolation with souls of the same ilk
for a very long time, since fewer opportunities to be reborn into
human bodies will arise for a lengthy period until the Earth
gradually repopulates. The ethnic uprisings are part of the same
pattern—a last-ditch effort to seize others' land when much of
it will be lost or laid waste with the Shift, so their efforts are in
vain. How much better for these warlike and evil ones to be
thinking of their souls' progress and taking advantage of these
final years to cleanse themselves of hatred and greed."

The Guides then addressed themselves to the second part of
my question, declaring: "As for the situation here after the
Shift, when so many souls are arriving at once, there are vastly

different levels in the spirit plane. Those who commit crimes of violence against innocent others will be at the lowest level and unable to attach themselves to those of higher spiritual development. Thus there will be no intermingling, although no rigid line is drawn. Like attracts like, and those of better character will find others like themselves at different strata. Just as a soul of little educational development would not seek the companionship of an Einstein or an Aristotle, so the ones you call the 'baddies' will not for a long time be fit or able to associate with those of higher spirituality."

It was a relief to learn that we will not be hobnobbing with murderers and terrorists after we pass into the spirit plane!

For the past several years the Guides have been predicting weather alterations that seem already to be coming to pass. In 1992 they wrote: "During the remainder of this decade there will be increasing weather change of a disastrous nature: storms, floods, increasing famine throughout the world due to these unsettled conditions, as well as continued spasmodic warfare. There is little that humankind can do to prevent the worsening weather, as it is a preparation for the Shift. Man could certainly prevent the war skirmishes and violence, but we do not see it being done."

In August of that year I had a rather eerie experience. Hurricane Andrew was headed straight for southern Florida, and since Bob was in a nursing facility located on somewhat higher ground than our beachfront condominium, I evacuated there to be with him. Spouses of other patients had done the same, and with no beds available to us, we sat up all night in a reception area. Soon power was lost, and with it television and radio reports of the impending catastrophe.

A couple of men had wisely brought along transistor radios, and as they held them to their ears they reported that Homestead, to the east, had been blasted into ruins, and the raging hurricane was now heading straight across the Everglades for Naples. We could see the palm trees outside, bending nearly double with the velocity of the winds, and suddenly I thought: How ridiculous of the lashing storm to be advancing on such a populated area, when by veering slightly to the southwest it could pass over virtually unoccupied areas of the peninsula.

It sounds a bit crazy, but I began mentally commanding the raging torrent to turn southwesterly. Over and over I gave it the directive, and that is exactly what happened with Hurricane Andrew. Naples lost only a few roofs and toppled trees as Andrew passed to the south of it, then harmlessly continued out to sea. I am not claiming credit for saving a city. I'm no Joan of Arc, but no doubt many thousands of others were silently merging their prayers with mine. I mention the episode only because of something that the Guides wrote shortly thereafter.

"We would like to tell you more about the times ahead," they wrote, "and the part that human will and endeavor can play in it. There are substantial ways that humankind can influence the elements, but they are unable to affect universal laws of the universe. Let us say that a storm is heading your way, and enough of you pray to divert its course into channels that will not cause widespread destruction of life and property. This can be done, as you have seen within your realms of experience. But when the time arrives for an adjustment to planet Earth in relationship with the universe, man will have little influence, if any, on that occurrence. It is a needed adjustment forced by universal laws. Our Creator foresees the necessity of adjustment in His divine plan, and man cannot influence such matters. Therefore, preparation is the better role for humankind, and as the time nears, many will begin adjusting to foreseen alterations in the Earth's surface."

The Guides added that "the U.S. president at that time will assist in preparing those who are willing to alter their lifestyles and locations, and other wise leaders abroad will also be alerting their own peoples and helping to prepare removals of populations" from areas most likely to be devastated. They declared that the "northern region of the North American continent will doubtless survive best [in the Western Hemisphere], and the temperature there will be much warmer after the Shift, whereas those land masses bordering the oceans will be most severely affected, due to tidal waves and shifting sands."

Whenever I resumed my sessions with the Guides, I pleadingly asked for more pleasant news about the coming years, but their messages were about as cheerful as the daily headlines in the press. On a typical day they wrote: "When the time approaches for the Shift, all will be familiar with omens and signs of the distress of the planet. These signs will include a slight wobbling that will register on scientific scales, and will be partially blamed on the denuding of forests and depletion of resources from beneath the Earth's surface. As the time nears for the cataclysmic alterations and realignments with the axis, some people will be feverishly packing to move to new locales that will be declared havens by the Walk-in president, who by then will be firmly in the saddle. He will already be inducing some industries and businesses to move to these relatively safe areas and stressing that the population shift necessitated by the approaching changes will supply ample reason for great numbers of people to seek employment and housing there. Wars will meanwhile still be fought in scattered areas of the strife-ridden globe, and no amount of warnings will cause the warring parties to heed the advice to forget their differences and begin helping one another to survive. As the fateful time approaches, earthquakes, flooding, drought, and other global catastrophes will already have decimated some areas, and rampant crime will make a farce of law and order. It is not a pretty picture, but that is what Earthlings are facing."

By now it should be apparent why I have been so reluctant to write another book. My readers clamor to know about the Guides' messages, but it's an axiom that everyone hates the messenger who brings bad tidings. The Guides do indeed have uplifting information about the predicted millennium that is to follow the Shift, but news of the immediate future is what people seem to want to know. Where, they ask, will they be safe?

At various times the Guides have replied as follows: "Many of those inland areas will indeed survive, but not all, because of the velocity of the winds and the destruction of buildings and trees that will send material flying in every direction. Along the seacoasts destruction will be more marked, since water will inundate much of the land; but mountains will shift, rivers will alter their courses, fields and streams will become intermingled, and an entirely new vista will emerge as the Earth stabilizes in its new position relative to the sun in its orbit. Masses of records will be destroyed, swept away by the waters or buried deep in the shifting earth, so it is good that special precautions are already being made to preserve many of these in various places, in duplicate and triplicate forms."

Another time they wrote: "Those who heed the safety warnings of the next president will do well to be prepared with foods that do not perish over a year's time, for the waters will recede slowly, and turmoil will prevail throughout the planet; not just in America, but everywhere, with some land areas enlarging, new lands emerging, and harvests available, while others will shrink as the waters cover the land for millennia. The Walk-in president will bring in with him more details on safe areas and plans to furnish survivors with livelihoods, but some will be heedless of his message, as fools have always been."

The Guides said the Walk-in has already "come to some prominence, although he is not currently viewed as a savior of the nation." Nonetheless, they continued, "He will providentially appear and announce such sensible plans for rescuing the economy and feeding the starving people that both parties will listen to him. No, it is not Ross Perot," they volunteered, "but one who has held a public office before he became a Walk-in."

After his election, according to the Guides, the new president will channel the energies of the people and prepare them for Earth changes, and most will cheerfully follow his recommendations. "The wasteful building up of areas that are known to be unsafe even now will virtually cease," they chided. "Californians will no longer continue to build expensive projects atop known rifts in the Earth's surface, expecting to be bailed out by the government when disaster unerringly follows. The same can be said for those who rebuild on vulnerable seashores and along the course of rivers that flood. It is a marvel on this side to see how foolishly such projects are undertaken, knowing the risks and still expecting to be bailed out by public money, when their own foolishness is exposed by flash floods, tremors, earthquakes, and the like."

The Guides foresee so many traumatic disasters that many will not care about surviving the Shift. "Thus not all will be thronging to the safer areas selected by the Walk-in president," they said. "But the younger ones in particular will welcome the opportunities being established there, with good job prospects and new housing away from shores and on higher land."

Describing the Walk-in president as "a dedicated, spiritual person," they declared that he will be a "godsend not only to Americans and Canadians, but to others throughout the planet, as he advises their governments and gives counsel to many."

When I asked the Guides, "Is there any way that we can avert the Shift or influence the timing?" they replied: "It will not be averted by anything humankind can do. It is in the hands of our Creator, who decides universal laws of truth and inevitability. If it is delayed beyond the period that we have named, it will be God's will and not man's. The timing is, of course, subject to natural laws, and if something that we have not foreseen intervenes for a period in delaying the Shift, it will be a higher universal law that prevails. Humankind is powerless to alter these universal trends."

I asked the Guides why the Shift was necessary and what it will accomplish, and they replied: "The Shift is necessary to cleanse the Earth of the evil that man has placed there. Also to rid the Earth of so many evil ones who have infiltrated the population. It will be swept nearly clean and raise the vibrations not only of the Earth but of its remaining inhabitants. As the Shift occurs the vibrations will be speeded up to a much higher frequency. The axis will remain steadfast, but the land and water masses will slip, not sideways, but in a rotating movement that will make the sun appear to stand still to those on Earth as the Shifting occurs."

I next asked what we as individuals can do spiritually to prepare ourselves for the Shift, and the Guides wrote: "Although humankind cannot avert the predestined Shift, we can prepare individually by prayer and meditation to feel a closeness with the whole, to love the Earth and its Creator. This will increase our own vibration and attune us to the forces of nature, so that we feel less the impact of the Earth's changed vibration, putting us in sync with it. Living a good life and loving others as brothers is an excellent way to begin: meditating on that daily at the same hour, and sending forth love instead of judgment, hate, or condemnation."

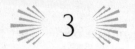

3

WHAT IS GOD'S PLAN?

Nearly everyone is familiar with the first verse of Genesis: "In the beginning God created the heaven and the earth," but what preceded that momentous event? How did it occur? Responding to my questions, the Guides wrote: "For the first trillions of years there was a void, a nothing, and an everything. It was all that there was—a sea of nothingness. Out of this void arose a Being so powerful that He began to command the nothingness to grow and to be. As the components of nothingness gradually learned to react to powerful commands, they began separating and spinning and evolving from nothingness into a mass of being.

"More eons passed, and as the mass separated itself through motion it became particles that gradually evolved into spinning balls, and then into an orbiting pattern around the mass. Thus the suns began to form, and as other particles spun off from the mass these became satellites of suns, forming planets; and as more and more particles obeyed the command they formed satellites around the planets. Time passed and the planets themselves began to divide into seas and lands, and after more eons the Earth itself began, and grew and developed. Life began as microorganisms and gradually developed a higher order of life, swimming, crawling, flying, and at last walking on [four] feet."

Another day the Guides took us a step farther, writing: "There was a time when all humans were consolidated in one energy, which many of us call God. We were all one. Then the mighty mass began to emit sparks, and each was separated from the others. All felt the oneness, but also the desire for exploration as separate entities, and as the Earth became populated by the lower species that we have mentioned, many of these sparks began to inhabit the bodies of animals, birds, fish, trees, and all living things. It was mystical and exciting, and for millennia these sparks or fragments of the Godhead continued to experiment, withdrawing from some life forms and entering others, to experience the novelty of life form. Some became so entangled in those forms that they refused to leave them, while others inspected, experienced, and moved on. Many stayed aloof from such physical manifestations, and some became what you would call angels, unrestrained by physical form and free to observe and assist others. This, then, was the beginning of souls, and as the species evolved, some became higher than others in mental and spiritual development.

"Then came the creation of the human form for those of higher development, but a few of them mingled sexually with those still inhabiting animal and bird forms. This retarded spiritual growth, because the Godhead had created an exclusive form for the human sparks to inhabit; and as we told you in *The World Before,* many progeny of these mismatches were born with tails, webbed feet, and other signs of crossbreeding. Thus even today there is an occasional physical throwback to that time."

Since they had mentioned angels in that discourse, I asked them to elaborate, and they declared: "As we have told you, angels are spirits who have not been born into flesh, but are filled with love and eager to help those in need. Everyone who is a believer in God's will attracts guardian angels, and there are many types of angels in various stages of development, just as there are humans on Earth and elsewhere." I asked if they are able to see angels, and they continued: "We do see angels, but they are not as worldly ones depict them. They are radiant beings not of human form who busy themselves with helpful acts of mercy or love. They indeed can assume human form when a sudden danger imperils an Earthling who is worth rescuing through warnings or helpful acts, but in their normal state they assume no particular form. They were not born into Earthly bodies, preferring to remain in the spirit realm and avoid the errors that we humans commit in Earthly bodies. No, they don't have wings or harps. They move with their thoughts, just as we do in this stage of spirit being."

It was intriguing to review the Guides' description of creation from "a void, a nothing, and an everything," but what, then, is God? Is He a force or a personal being to whom we can pray and from whom we can expect help? I put the question in writing, and the Guides replied: "God is everything. He is the creative force and the glue that holds the universe together. He is also a personal counselor, since a part of Him is in you and every living thing. God is all! If we follow the true dictates of our own conscience, the divine spark, we will not go wrong. God does hear prayers, including the ones that you pray for us in the spirit plane. Don't ever doubt it, Ruth. This is the essential truth that guides us all."

Still curious, I pressed the question at a subsequent session, asking if anyone in the plane where the Guides are ever sees God. They replied: "In the spirit plane where we are we do not see someone called God, but we are aware of His being permeating every conceivable dot of space. We are His creations, and He is everything. We use the generic pronoun 'He' to

simplify, but God has no sex. Sex was created in order to people the Earth—humans, beasts, birds, and all manner of crea-
tures and vegetation—but God is the Whole. He is neither
male nor female; He is the all. We do not seek proof of His
being because we see it in everything and feel the magnificence
of His spiritual being. God is good. He is the light and the
darkness, the rain and the sunshine, the all-knowing and all-
caring Creator of all things. You are wondering about Satan.
Yes, he too was created in God's goodness, but after all beings
were granted free will he fell, just as the 'baddies' on Earth fall
from the light."

This latter comment naturally piqued my curiosity, and at
another session I asked for an elaboration on Satan. This is
what they wrote: "Satan was among the hierarchy of angels
created long before humankind came into being on Earth. He
was a radiant being, so we are told, and as close as one can be
to God. The angels, like the sparks that became human beings,
were given free will and provided companionship to God.
Satan wanted to be the all to his Creator. He resented that
other light-beings also shared God's love, and as jealousy
began, so did that evil emotion permeate the thinking of others, until God finally had to cast out Satan because he was pol-
luting the heavenly abode. When God eventually created
human bodies on planet Earth, Satan saw an opportunity for

revenge, or at least a way to demonstrate his power, and he initiated the temptations that have forever since plagued humankind."

While this material was coming through, I received a telephone call from Betty Mills, a close friend, who, sounding rather perplexed, asked, "Ruth, do you believe that God and Jesus are the same? That Jesus is actually God?"

Surprised, I replied that I considered Jesus to be the Son of God, but not God Himself. "That has always been my assumption, too," she continued, "but at my Bible class this morning we were told that God and Jesus are identical."

Aware that Betty attends a weekly Bible class at her Presbyterian church, I wondered how Presbyterians could then explain the Apostles' Creed, which they repeat at Sunday services. After all, it begins, "I believe in God the Father Almighty, maker of heaven and earth, and in Jesus Christ His only Son our Lord, Who was conceived by the Holy Ghost, born of the Virgin Mary. . . ."

At my next session with the Guides I posed Betty's question, and they wrote: "Jesus was created by God in His image, as we all were, and are. Jesus was a highly developed soul who had proven His worth through many previous incarnations, and when He was baptized, the Christ spirit descended into Him and He became Jesus the Christ. This Christ spirit has existed since the beginning of time, and will return in the next century to another perfected being, but Jesus the man is no more God than are any of us. It is the Christ spirit that is an integral part of 'God the Father,' as He is called. The so-called Holy Ghost is the spirit of God, which exists within all of us who are seeking a return to the essence of God. It is the knowingness within each person. More than just the conscience within us, it is the very essence of the Christ Spirit. It is our enduring link with the Godhead, the 'still small voice' that links us to the essence of the Creator, the divine part of our being."

Recalling that Jesus reportedly once said, "I and the Father are one," I asked at a subsequent session how that could be if they were not identical. The Guides replied: "That is simply not a correct interpretation of biblical passages. As plainly stated in what we call the Good Book, Jesus referred to Himself as the Son of God, and we are all the children of God, inasmuch as He created us all. Jesus was endowed with the Christ spirit at the time of His baptism by John the Baptist, and thereby became an integral part of the Godhead. Very few others have received that special Christ spirit, but it is not unique in the world. It is a Oneness bestowed by God on perfect human beings who are lifted up to the highest pinnacle in eternity, but they are different from God the Creator of the universe. We are unable to express it more clearly at this time."

4

EARTH CHANGES

How happy I am to report that the Guides are now much more optimistic in their prognostications for us! Not only do they see the Shift delayed, but also they perceive it now as a much less destructive force. In September 1998 they wrote: "The damage looks to be considerably less than we earlier foresaw, due to the improved spirituality of Earthlings. America's East Coast will be less damaged, except for the tearing up of beaches and some construction, and Western Europe will be much less battered than we foresaw earlier, because there too the Europeans are helping one another and trying to follow the rules of God. It will not be as catastrophic as we had feared, thanks to the uplifting of humankind and an indulgent Creator."

They added that New York City and parts of California will

survive (as opposed to previous predictions) because of man's improving spiritual growth, "with so many becoming interested in the whys of life. So many more are curious and delving now than at the time we began our work." They continued, "It is a new age, a new era of enlightenment, and your books have played an important role in advancing that period and awakening slumbering souls to the new reality."

I asked the Guides about their mistaken prediction two decades ago of a world war in the late 1980s, and they replied: "That war was forestalled by the returnees of the Hundred Years' War and the Walk-ins who worked together to turn away the Satanic impulses that would have plunged you into a horrendous war. We foresaw many dying in that era and not yet the good results that would incur from those forces combined to forestall war. So it was foreseeing multiple deaths from AIDS that led us to that error. Sorry about it, but thank heavens it was an error. We do not foresee another war in the near future, and after the new millennium begins there will be no major ones."

Prodded again to explain why the predicted Shift is being delayed, the Guides patiently continued: "It was delayed because, as we told you, humans' awareness has improved these last decades, and the need to cleanse the Earth of evil beings is less pertinent. Not that all evil is erased, by any means, but because man's functioning by God's laws is improving. We cannot give an exact date for the Shift, but it depends on continued development of man's spirit, and we did not see it happening until after the Walk-in president is in place, which will not occur for ten to fifteen years yet. The important thing is for people to abide by God's laws and love one another, thus speeding up their own vibration to match the increased vibration of the Earth itself. All is in speed stimulus and nothing is to be feared, as life goes on for all."

What about our infrastructure, such as hospitals, libraries, museums, electric power plants, and computers? Will these survive the Shift? The Guides replied that much of it will indeed survive, although the most important preparation during the next ten to fifteen years should be the duplication or triplication of valuable records to be stored in various safer areas. They said that electric power will indeed be knocked out, but soon restored. They added that after the Shift, democracy will spread throughout the world "and the new breed will make remarkable improvement on the process, without curtailing freedom. There will be fewer have-nots and more abundant times as the Earth recovers from its wounds, so it's a wonderfully bright picture in the new millennium."

I interrupted their sequence to ask the Guides about the expected computer problems at the dawn of the year 2000, when computers will not be able to distinguish between the years 1900 and 2000 because of our long-standing habit of omitting the "19" before our datings. They said soothingly that "we foresee no particularly devastating problem, as souls from this side will plant into the minds of brilliant mathematicians in physical being the way to repair the damage. It will not amount to the major problem now foreseen by Earthlings," they concluded.

The Guides also sounded upbeat about other Earthly worries. They said AIDS will be swept away after the Shift, and "we do not see a great problem with Ebola and strep—just the usual pangs that plague humankind. After the Shift Earthlings will be so open to this sphere where we are that they can far better cope with medicinal and all other problems."

Responding to specific questions, they wrote, "We do not see the man-made biological weapons unleashed at the time of the Shift, and they will be destroyed afterward. The same with nuclear weapons. We don't see them bursting open and causing havoc, but safely destroyed in the millennium of peace that follows. We see women coming into their own after the Shift, with wise leaders erasing purdah and opening education to both sexes and all races. What a difference that will make to the world, with women coming to the fore! The terrorists will disappear as new leadership renounces their efforts after the

Shift, but they will continue to present problems until then. The world will be so much better then that people living in the new millennium will look back on these times and shake their heads in wonderment at the current inability of humankind to live peacefully together.

"This turbulence today has long been foreseen for wiping the slate clean of this old millennium and preparing for the better new one, when hatreds will begin to die out, as the Atlanteans do also. Fundamentalism is a hangover from the days when zealots said, 'Believe as I do or you are wrong.' This too will fade away as there is greater fellowship and love between people who are all parts of the God Being and realize it. The plagues are not visited by God on humans, but come from their own karma when they played fast and loose with what is right. They too will practically vanish with the Shift.

"The Shift will be such a cleansing force that blacks and whites will forget their strife over color and realize that inside they are all one: all a part of the Godhead. The same with Muslims and Jews, who are all one race but divided over ownership of a small piece of Earth's surface. With the Shift they will realize that the Earth belongs to God, not man, and no one has exclusive rights to any slab of it. Yes, the Shift is not to be dreaded, but anticipated, as it will heal the suffering Earth and its population, and love will be rediscovered."

The Guides repeated that AIDS will begin to disappear soon after the Shift, and since the HIV virus that often develops into AIDS appeared first among certain homosexual groups, I asked: "How is homosexuality viewed in the spirit plane, and is the trait carried over from previous lifetimes?" I was recalling that in *Here and Hereafter* the Guides indicated that many of those men today who call themselves gay had been women in several recent incarnations, and had not fully adjusted to the sex change, even though they had chosen their present gender to round out their spiritual development.

Replying to my question, they wrote: "As to homosexuality, there has always been that tendency, almost from the beginning. There were other so-called Adams and Eves and their progeny, besides the original family mentioned in the Bible, and some strains were more prone than others to prefer a same-sex orientation. As viewed from this plane, it is not regarded as a sin so long as the parties are in agreement, and no one is lured into that cohabitation by others. Yes, that desire is sometimes carried over from one lifetime to another, but not unless the soul truly prefers that way of life and desires to continue it. The only cardinal sin attached to it, as far as we can observe, is the luring or forcing of others into a way of life that may ultimately be offensive to them."

Since my books are circulated throughout the English-speaking world and have been translated into numerous foreign languages, I receive fan mail from every continent. Most of the questions from those correspondents naturally concern their own areas: Will it be safe in Australia? New Zealand? South Africa? Asia, or wherever?

Sometimes I ask about a specific area in order to answer such a query. I do not recall what prompted a question about Tasmania, but in shuffling through my accumulated mass of automatic writing, I note that in 1990 the Guides wrote: "Tasmania will survive until the Shift, when waters will indeed pour over much of the land area, but it will grow considerably in size after the waters recede." Where is Tasmania? I had to resort to an atlas to remember that it is an island south of Australia.

Another day I asked about the Clinton administration's handling of the bloody warfare then raging in the former Yugoslavia, and my spirit mentors replied: "Its handling of that situation is not too bad, as it is apparently impossible to wipe out the ancient hatreds and ethnic rivalries there. The Shift will be the answer to that, as the survivors forget about their bitter rivalries in the struggle to cope with the new environment and altered climatic changes."

I wanted to know about Asia, and the answer came: "The Asian portion of the globe will be somewhat smaller than it is today, as parts of the coastal areas vanish. India will survive as a smaller peninsula. The deserts of China will blossom again, but that country will not entirely be spared. Vast areas of it will

be underwater, and the population will, of course, be decimated, as will the Earth's population as a whole. Those who
survive will throw off the yoke of Communist dictatorship as
they struggle to make the land tenable again and to feed the
survivors, but strongmen will again arise in China, and their
personal ambitions will have to be curbed, as they will be. The
young survivors will demand leading roles and will refuse to be
trod upon by such leaders."

I pressed the Guides to tell us what they foresee for other
areas of the planet, and they responded: "In Australia, except
for unsafe coastal areas at the time of the Shift, the continent
will vastly enlarge, and the outback area will become fertile and
pleasant.

"In Africa deserts will be flooded with water for a time, and
then will become some of the most fertile areas of the Earth,
since they have long lain fallow. Parts of South America will
also bloom, although temperature changes there will be varied.
Some of the Atlantic seaboard of Western Europe will vanish
beneath the sea, so every attempt should be made to preserve
records of its high culture. We will deal with other alterations
at a later time."

A "later time" finally arrived, and they volunteered: "Some
of Japan will survive—the higher areas—but not all of it, and
Australia and New Zealand will increase in size. We've recently

told you about India, China, and Africa, and the latter will be verdant—perhaps the least damaged of all the continents. There will be widespread damage in the Mediterranean area. Russia will become warmer, and the Urals will be a particularly safe area, as it looks from here."

Addressing the Western Hemisphere, they declared that both the North and South American coasts will be affected due to the ferocity of tidal waves during the Shift. Some of the seacoast areas will gradually come back, they continued, "bearing the scars of the devastation and inundation by salt water. The mountainous areas will be safest, but some of them will also undergo severe damage, due to the shifting and tilting of land masses."

Central America, they continued, "will suffer enormous damage due to its proximity to the seas on both coasts, but South America will enlarge. It will, however, be colder than at present, since the South Pole will be roughly centered in the extreme southern part of that continent."

At this point in the writing of this book, I evacuated to a more inland hotel, because Hurricane Georges was headed straight for Naples on Florida's west coast. The Guides had already told me that they foresaw no hurricanes lambasting Naples during this season, and when I asked whether I should follow the official advice and evacuate, the Guides said that was up to me, but, referring to my deceased husband, they broke in to say, "Bob says, 'Stay put.'" How I wish that I had followed his advice instead of listening to friends and TV warnings: Even as I moved, I began trying the same tactics I had used during Hurricane Andrew, mentally commanding Georges to turn out into the Gulf of Mexico instead of bearing along the land toward Naples. That is exactly what occurred, and we emerged almost unscathed. After my return home, the Guides wrote: "Welcome back again. That was a valuable preparation for the Shift: to organize what to have ready to take with you and how to plan ahead."

They reiterated previous forecasts that Florida will survive mainly as a few small islands after the Shift, and that California will already have lost some of its land, due to earthquake activity. They said Texas coastal areas and those of Mexico and Central America will be hazardous and should be avoided during the Shift. "Eventually some of these areas will reemerge," they added, "but are not to be considered habitable during and for a time after the Shift."

On a more cheerful note, they wrote: "But as we have long foreseen, ancient Lemuria will rise again in some rather large portions of the Pacific, and a part of Atlantis will also rise between North America and Africa."

Convinced that some readers will be alarmed by such predictions, I asked the Guides for suggestions to lull their fears, and they declared: "There are those who right now are packing up to leave their familiar surroundings because of fear of the Shift. Their haste is unnecessary. There will be ample warnings, as we have said, and preparations made for an influx of those wishing to survive in the flesh, at various spots that are likely survival areas. It is unseemly to pull up whole families now from schools and jobs unless good situations await them in new surroundings. We would suggest that everyone be calm and tarry awhile to see what develops with the future planning by the new president. Meanwhile, gather seeds for all types of climates, staple foods, and hand tools that do not require electricity."

Musing about their remarks, I felt a bit mutinous. It is easy enough for spirits who are not treading on Earth with physical feet to say, "Don't worry." They can flit about and remain above it all. What about the rest of us?

Apparently reading my thoughts, the Guides chided: "Let us say that it will not be frightening for those who realize that life goes on and on and on. Only those who live for today, or who are frightened of losing their material possessions, will be bothered by what we have to say. They too can profit by it, since it should help to awaken them to the reality of the great truth: There is no such thing as death."

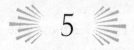

5

HUMAN PREPAREDNESS

The Guides want us to know about the twenty-first century, the beginning of an era of enlightenment, but they want to unravel the future in proper sequence, and to do so they must first discuss the Shift itself and its immediate aftermath. On more than one occasion I have asked them how we could prepare ourselves for what is to come.

They opened our discussion by observing that "the auras and awareness of humans are changing and developing so rapidly that they will be ready for the changes that lie ahead. The world seems to have speeded up, although actually it is not the physical but the spiritual world that is making the leaps in advancement. Just as mere youngsters are now able to handle computer problems that are difficult for adults, so their more subtle abilities are making rapid progress.

"As the time nears for the Shift, there will be an entire array of seemingly new beings ready to move to the forefront," the Guides said. "These young ones will be the leaders after the Shift, and a great time it will be for the advancement of humanity. Make no mistake, that time is coming, and those in flesh are rapidly being prepared for it, so there is nothing to fear. Those who are out of the flow will probably not survive long in the new age, but they will be ready to go into spirit and glad to leave the rebuilding to younger and abler beings."

I asked how humans can get into the flow, and they wrote: "Take yourself as an example. You are often exhausted because you have not learned how to make yourself a part of the energy field—the flow. Try it often, prone on the bed or floor, or even in your lounge chair. Feel yourself slipping headfirst into the vortex of energy above, below, and all around you. Feel yourself becoming part of it, and drawing it in as you return to the normal state. Everyone can do it, and this will help more than anything, emotionally and physically. Do this exercise twice daily to merge with the universal energy."

Vaguely recalling that one of my previous books contained a chapter on the flow, I finally located it in *Strangers Among Us*. "The entire cosmos is energy," the Guides had written. "It's not just composed of energy, it *is* energy, and since we are infinitesimal parts of the cosmos, we too are energy. Therefore, when you say that you are tired, you are simply saying that you are out of tune with the universal energy, the cosmic flow. Get into it and swim. Submerge yourself in it. Feel yourself as a pulsating, living part of the universe." As usual, I had neglected to follow through on their advice.

One day recently a friend, Dr. Mary Jane Ledyar, who is a clinical psychologist, asked if I would question the Guides about the role of organized religions in the new age. Do they help people to become more spiritual, and will the separate denominations continue after the Shift?

The Guides initiated their reply by writing: "Jesus Christ founded no religion, as you know. Christianity was unregulated and had no set rules until the Roman Empire adopted it as its official religion and the Catholic Church was organized. Over the centuries it gradually became so formalized that Martin Luther and then others rose up against its rigorous edicts, and divisions of Christianity sprang up throughout the world. All of that is history, of course.

"The main thing to remember is that organized religions have helped many people to become more spiritual and to live lives that they consider to be in keeping with the Golden Rule. 'Organized' religion is not for everyone, nor is it a necessity in seeking spiritual progress. Each of us is born with a knowledge of right and wrong. Some of the children have this bred out of them by rascally parents or companions, but the innate knowledge is there: the Golden Rule that is far older than Christianity and bespeaks the fundamental principle that we should not do unto others what we would not want done to ourselves.

"That is the basic philosophy of all spiritual speakers, and has not been improved upon through many millennia. At the time of the Shift this will be a very important precept, as people try to help others survive, if they wish to do so in the physical sense. That attempt at helping others is also a one-way ticket to progression in the spirit plane, for no act of good or of evil is lost in the balance wheel on this side."

I asked if organized religions would continue after the Shift, and the Guides replied that there will be far fewer divisions, "but spiritual realization will become much deeper as those who survive in flesh realize that there is purpose in their continuance in physical form, and that God's majesty is realized in every living thing. The animals that survive will be tenderly nurtured, as will the birds and fish. Some will furnish sustenance for the hungry, true, but there will exist a oneness that forbids slaughter for mere sport."

And what about those communities of like-minded individuals that are often labeled cults? The Guides said that some of them are splendid, providing a way to worship together in unity, "but others are armed to the teeth and so ferocious that they will wish to kill hungry wanderers after the Shift. This defies every vestige of spirituality, and their continuance is short upon the Earth. The survivors who invest in love are the ones who will help to replenish the Earth, and as new souls enter physical body, they will be joyously welcomed as gifts from the Creator."

Lily added: "Many will be well prepared to survive in physical body, although none will know exactly where to locate for safety. It will be like a giant roulette wheel, where some are saved and others are gone. All souls will, of course, survive, but there will be no trace of many bodies or former dwellings. Those who physically survive will be so astounded by the narrow escape from seeming disaster that good feelings will prevail for a time, until bands of hungry homeless begin descending on areas that seem well stocked with food and other necessities. Then the bestial nature of some survivors will emerge as they attempt to plunder and even kill to satisfy their own wants at the expense of others. Those who try to protect their own hoards will be in great danger, and havoc will result in these areas. But some will gladly share."

On another occasion, the Guides informed me: "All should be preparing for the Shift by assembling food that will not spoil, and thinking of where they wish to live if they want to survive in physical form. After the Shift, new ways will be developed for producing sustenance, and perhaps freeing

Earthlings from the routine of food preparation three times a day. It is a beautiful time that we see ahead after the Earth is cleansed by the Shift and virtually reinhabited by advanced souls, not only the ones who survive there, but those who are allowed to be born into the new vehicles—the future mothers. There is nothing to fear. It will be a time of peace, tranquility, and understanding, as well as love for one another."

6

PETS AND WILDLIFE

The Guides vigorously deny that the turn of the century will presage the "end of the world," as certain doomsayers have prophesied. Instead, they foresee a joyous era beyond, a veritable Garden of Eden without the snake. That made me wonder about the other beings with whom we share the Earth.

Introducing the subject of wild animals, I asked what will happen to them and to household pets at the time of the Shift. The Guides replied that many people will have taken their dogs and cats with them as they move to safer areas, but wild animals will face the same fate as humans, if in unsafe areas.

"When the Shift occurs, many of the sleek, woolly, and wonderful animals will perish, but many others will survive into the new age and flourish, as man ceases to hunt them except in desperation for food," they wrote. "Fish will have a better chance of survival, although many will be swept onto land by the tidal waves and perish. Birds will also have good odds, since they are able to lift themselves from the Earth as the Shift occurs, although winds and water will take their toll. Birds and fish will find new feeding grounds as lands now beneath the sea emerge, bringing new shorelines and rich proteins to nourish all forms of life."

The Guides observed that some forms of wildlife seem already to sense radical changes ahead and to be seeking safer environments.

A friend wanted to know if our pets have souls, and the Guides replied: "Our pets are, as we told you in an earlier book, a part of group souls, and as animals progress to higher levels, they do not become humans, but evolve within their own species: for as you know, we have many of them here, and they too want to be with more highly developed humans, as well as in their own species. It is a beautiful plan, and nothing is to be feared as long as one lives up to the ideals set by the sainted ones."

Stressing that all will survive, whether or not in physical form, they made this interesting observation about species that have become extinct: "We have many of them here that no longer inhabit the Earth, yet are preserved for later introduction there, or perhaps to other planetary systems."

Intrigued by how this could be accomplished without progenitors present to propagate, they replied that "we are unaware of the process of how, but it will be done." I asked what will happen to animals who are in zoos, and they responded: "A few animals may escape, but not enough to create big problems, and the others will be carefully tended by loving caretakers, as they are during hurricanes and other storms. Animals are rather rapidly evolving in consciousness, just as are humans. It's the speeded-up reality that we are now seeing, and man and beast will be much abler to communicate with each other through ESP, just as you did with the peacock in Cuernavaca, Mexico."

That reminder brought back the eerie feeling that I experienced when my brother and a friend were visiting Bob and me, and we took them to a popular restaurant in Cuernavaca, which was situated in an elaborate garden through which peacocks strutted. Always before, a few of them had spread their lovely tails in a fan shape, but on this occasion they simply dragged their heavy tails behind them. I was eager for my brother to see the beauty of the usual demonstration, so I finally walked to the middle of the garden and stared one of the peacocks in the eye. I mentally explained to him that I wished to show him off and urged him to spread his tail. We eyed each other steadily, and after I had repeated the mental request several times, he obligingly spread his beautiful tail. Other guests clapped, and all ended happily, but I shivered at the feeling that I had been inside his mind.

Many readers throughout recent years have written to ask what becomes of our beloved pets when they die. Since the Guides were now discussing animals, it seemed a good time to ask Bob if he had seen any of our pets since passing into spirit. For half a century we had always had one or two dogs at a time, until moving some years ago to a condominium that bars pets.

"They are here and they recognize me," Bob responded. "But it's been a long time, as you know, and they've made other connections. Muffy [our last one] is the one I see around me the most, and Princess, of course. The others were more your dogs than mine, so they aren't here too often."

Musing about this afterward, I realized that he was right. Our female dogs seemed to prefer Bob, and the male ones followed me. Opposites apparently continue to attract, even in the spirit plane.

7

ALIEN VISITATIONS

Mysterious crop circles appearing overnight in random fields throughout the planet! Sightings of UFOs on every continent! Cattle mutilations! Alien experimentation with human beings who claim to have undergone minor operations or the removal of their sperm or ova! Television and newspapers are rife with lurid accounts of such strange occurrences. What is going on here?

I am fascinated by the Guides' response. "When man first came into the Earth as experimenters, trying out the bodies of animals, birds, and fish of the seas, he was doing exactly what the aliens are doing today, and have been doing for a long time—trying out a new environment and Earthly vehicles as a test of their powers. Man was also a space being, as is everything that moves and breathes and has being.

"Some of man's experiments in inhabiting animal forms turned out disastrously, even as some of the space people's experiments do on Earth today. None is perfect, and although their chief reason for coming to Earth is to observe the upcoming shift of the Earth on its axis, nonetheless the aliens would like to help humans survive it, by following the means that they themselves are using—to project themselves in thought forms to other planets and to safer areas on the Earth's surface. Although the visiting aliens are not entirely altruistic, and some are purely of scientific bent, desiring to experiment with and examine Earth's inhabitants, nevertheless they do not actually intend harm. It is increasingly dangerous on Earth to cross a street, to fly in a plane, or to ride in an automobile, so why be particularly afraid of space beings who may visit you from time to time?"

Wow! That was thought-provoking, to say the least!

A substantial portion of our population dismisses the possibility of alien visitations as tabloid journalism, and our government continues to deny, or remains mum on, reported sightings and alien spacecraft that have allegedly landed or crashed. My Guides have long insisted that such occurrences are real, and when I now asked if there is continuing activity of space aliens, they responded: "Yes, and it is increasing constantly throughout the globe. The aliens are studying conditions and experimenting with animals and people in order to preserve the Earth's species on other planets and in other galaxies, because of the impending Shift. They literally mean no harm. They are trying to preserve the human race and species of animals, vegetation, and other forms of life that would be extremely valuable to reintroduce into a stabilized Earth, or to other planets that can sustain those life forms. That's what they are testing for now, and Earthlings should not be alarmed by their visits. They seldom interfere with humans who are unwilling to take the risk. They are extremely selective and want only to help. Those aliens who come and go from Earth are from highly developed technological systems, and although some of these aliens might not be to the liking of you and others, they are scientists of the highest order."

Recalling pictures of aliens allegedly encountered by human beings, I agreed that it might be difficult to like them, although I adored Steven Spielberg's depiction of lovable little E.T.

I next queried the Guides about the crop circles in England, the United States, and elsewhere, which when photographed from the air appear to be marvelously intricate designs. They said that although a few are obviously hoaxes perpetrated by human beings, "some were indeed made by extraterrestrials who are leaving messages for other outer-space beings. The beautifully formed ones have been done by scientific methods not yet understood on Earth. As we look ahead we see a speeding-up of scientific discovery on planet Earth as minds are opened to the probability of visitations by outer-space beings, so this should quicken the discoveries that will lead to further preparation for the Shift and the millennium to follow."

Since the Guides indicate that advanced space beings are already aware of the impending shift of the Earth on its axis, I asked what will cause the Shift, and they replied: "It will occur when the ice builds up to the highest degree at the poles, and the imbalance leads to a slip of the Earth on its side. We do not see collision with a comet or stellar body contributing to the slip. The teetering will begin shortly before the event, and instruments will be able to record the wobble, but when it occurs it will be so rapid that an eye will scarcely have time to blink. There is no way that humankind can prevent it, as the time is overripe for another Shift."

The Guides stressed that there are other life forms on many planets "both within and without your galaxy." They said that the same God created all, but different kinds of life forms developed in various areas of the universe. "Some of the planets are vastly more advanced than Earth and were created much earlier," they wrote. "Their beings do not resemble the human form, and some are vastly more developed in science and technology than Earthlings. Other planets trail behind Earth in their development, but it is the advanced ones whose inhabitants have been visiting Earth, or at least keeping tabs on it. Many are aware of the upcoming Shift through their advanced measurements, and that has piqued their interest, just as Earthlings are stirred with excitement about the bombardment of Jupiter by remnants of a fragmented comet."

Curious about their spiritual development, I asked the Guides whether beings on other planets had their own Christs, and they replied with unaccustomed modesty, "That is unknown to us in this stage of our development."

Several times in recent years, my Guides have indicated that aliens will be instrumental in rescuing some Earthlings who could not otherwise survive the Shift. I now asked them for further information on that intriguing subject.

According to the Guides, those who survive the Shift will be numbered in the millions, but nothing like today's population on Earth. "Aliens will be around to help for brief stints but will not be able to stay for longer periods without again returning to their own atmospheres." The Guides reminded us that some aliens already occupy human bodies, having arrived through the Walk-in process, but since they discussed that topic at length in *Aliens Among Us,* I did not pursue it here. Instead, I asked whether aliens from other planetary systems will want to live on Earth after the Shift, and they replied: "After the Shift there will be a scramble for available bodies of new-born babies, due to the decimated population. Therefore, they may not be available to any except souls of good ethics who have more recently lived on Earth and want to return to replenish it and help with the restructuring of their home planet."

The Guides assert that one method of rescue for physical survivors will be "the lifting off by means of spaceships that will need to navigate around the Earth for several days during the turmoil of the Shift, until stability returns to the orbiting planet." They say that during the orbiting, the rescued Earth-lings "will be infused with healing energies so that they can assist those injured by falling debris and the like, and they will be given knowledge of where to establish new abodes and how to meet the immediate needs of survival, until seeds can be planted and crops harvested."

Apparently wishing to sum up what they had recounted to date, they wrote: "Aliens from outer space will be watching with keen interest and readying vehicles to help take some off the Earth before the Shift, and many of these ships will simply stay in orbit for the necessary time before returning those beings to Earth. Others will take their human cargo directly to other planetary systems through a process not yet understood in your sphere. Those who elect to return to Earth at a later time will doubtless be allowed to do so, but some will choose to remain in their new environment. Let us emphasize that this is not a wholesale evacuation project, but a careful selection of those who are deserving of perpetuation in bodily form or who have remarkable talents to contribute during the rebuilding of Earth's environs."

(While retyping this passage, I smiled to myself to discover that the lilting tune "You better be good, you better be nice . . . Santa Claus is coming to town" was running through my thoughts. Perhaps it was telling me something!)

Now comes the part that boggles my mind. The Guides began the discussion by asserting: "We would have you visualize a shining star high in the heavens that appears to flicker and almost beckon to you. That planetary object will become a safe haven for many of those who will be spending some time before and after the Shift in a different form. This is not to say that their physical bodies will be transported there, but since human bodies are composed of energy and the molecules that make up all things that appear to be solids, those molecules will be reassembled after having been disassembled shortly before the Shift. That energy will be preserved on the planetary object mentioned above, until Earth is sufficiently stabilized after the Shift to support a life normally."

Baffled by such a ridiculous-sounding procedure, I asked if they were speaking of what the Bible calls the "Rapture." They replied that it could be compared to the Rapture, but not as ordinarily depicted. "Those whose molecules are dissolved will simply disappear and their soul or essence will be transported and reassembled elsewhere, as we mentioned earlier. It is within your own galaxy and is an extremely luminous object. The souls transported there will be aware of their new surroundings and of one another, but will form little attachment to the holding area. They are the ones who will have a great deal to do with the spiritual rebuilding of Earth—not so much the rebuilding of things as of ideas and realizations. They will blend easily with those who withstood the Shift, and all will work together for the furtherance of humankind's development."

This was definitely over my head, but a few days later I gamely asked how many would be selected for that weird journey and whether aliens would execute this unheard-of maneuver. As calmly as if they were discussing yesterday's news, the Guides replied: "They will be numbered in the hundreds of thousands, and aliens will indeed assist. But it is a basic law of physics that will make the dissolution and reassemblage possible. These are souls who are considered invaluable because of their spiritual ways and their knowledge of Earth's environment, so they will be exceedingly useful on their return, and will be reinvigorated so that the older ones will be up to the task. They are the ones who have earned the right to survive and to return in order to contribute their wisdom and talents."

Hmmmmmmmm. I began to wish that I had studied physics instead of the arts while I had the chance in college.

8

THE WALK-IN PRESIDENT

The Guides have long predicted that a Walk-in would become president of the United States and would be of inestimable value in preparing us for the cataclysmic shift of the Earth. When Bill Clinton and George Bush became the nominees of the major political parties in 1992, and Ross Perot declared his independent candidacy, the Guides asserted that none of them was the individual who would play that crucial role in history.

"Yes, it will be a man," they continued, "and as we told you many years ago, there will be no woman president of the United States during the twentieth century."

Readers of my previous books will recall that long-ago prophecy, and also the accompanying one in which they foretold that soon Great Britain would choose a woman prime minister "who is a Tory." This seemed far-fetched at the time, since few Americans were even aware of a Tory member of Parliament named Margaret Thatcher, but within two years she became the first British woman prime minister.

In the 1991 message they further wrote: "The Walk-in whose name is already familiar to many but not to all Americans will undergo the transformation within the next two or three years, and thereby be ready to assume the helm. His reputation will already have been established under the present identity, but many will remark the alteration in him shortly thereafter."

The following day they declared that "during the next few years there will be tremendous alterations in the weather patterns, so that these recent years will be regarded in retrospect as idyllic." Continuing their predictions of earthquakes, floods, and "tornadoes that will rip through the heartland of America," they added: "That is when the Walk-in will become exceedingly prominent, as he will by then have undergone a revolution from within. His candidacy will be announced, and he will be overwhelmingly elected, as he advises people on safe moves and prepares to set up government-endorsed housing and businesses in sections of America that seem most likely to survive the Shift. Meanwhile, leaders in Europe and Asia will be casting about for similar projects and seeking advice from this American president."

From time to time I sought to know the identity of the promised Walk-in, but the Guides have consistently refused to divulge it. They did occasionally drop hints, as if we were playing a guessing game on *Jeopardy!* In May of 1993 they said that the individual "is already in office, in a rather unpublicized position, and will be assembling a fine set of solutions before his presidential race."

In January of 1994 the Guides were still reporting that the mysterious president-to-be had not completed the soul exchange. Referring to the body's present identity, they said: "The future president is now prominent but has not yet become a Walk-in. That will occur when he suddenly awakens to the futility of politics and the power game and will surrender his soul to the spirit plane, making way for his own replacement. When this occurs, many will be amazed at the alteration in his personality and goals. Some will scoff that it is for political purposes, but it will actually be the Walk-in who has taken over and who plunges into the task of preparing people for dramatic alterations in Earth and weather patterns."

Another day they tantalized me by writing: "His advent into body will occur shortly, so watch for hints of a rather radical change in a fairly prominent man. The Walk-in will be full of ideas and plans as he enters the new body that is already well established politically. He foresees from this side what needs to be done to alert people and prepare the safe areas for habitation by large numbers."

In the spring I had a succession of houseguests, which kept me so busy—and exhausted—that I virtually abandoned the automatic writing. Then I broke my toe, and it was so painful that I decided to cancel a long-scheduled visit to Greta Woodrew, a cherished friend who wanted me to speak at a seminar she was conducting in the verdant mountains of North Carolina.

But the Guides had different plans for me. I was definitely to make the trip, they said, even though I was physically exhausted and hobbling on a battered toe. The visit would inspire me, they declared, to begin writing the book that they had been urging on me for so long.

The last thing that I wanted to contemplate, in my weakened state, was writing another book, but my Guides are very persuasive. I went to North Carolina, changing planes en route, and by the time Greta and her husband, Dick, met my plane in Asheville, the pain in my toe was excruciating. After all, I had walked through what seemed miles of concrete corridors at airports in Fort Myers, Charlotte, and Asheville to reach my destination.

We had a pleasant evening's chat, and I slept well. The next morning after breakfast, Greta inquired how my toe was feeling, and with some surprise I replied that I hadn't noticed it yet. "I sent it healing last night," she said with a smile.

I had momentarily forgotten about Greta's healing powers, even though I had read about them in her two books, *On a Slide of Light* and *Memories of Tomorrow.* I knew her simply as a good friend who had the ability to bend untouched forks and spoons and as a fellow explorer in the psychic field. Thus reminded of her other talent, I expressed the hope that she would also send me some healing energy before my departure.

She did so, and skeptic that I have always been, I now take the witness stand to attest: My toe never again pained me, and I returned with such renewed energy that I began preparation for this book. The Guides never say "I told you so," but they seemed pleased with the resumption of our regular sessions.

And something else had happened while I was nursing my own problems. The exchange of the souls had apparently occurred between the Walk-in president-to-be and his predecessor, because in July 1998 they wrote: "Now for the Walk-in. His name is recognizable to you, although you do not know him. He has been in the government in some very good spots heretofore, and now that he has become a Walk-in he will begin to energize that body and formulate plans for meeting the crises facing America and the world. The substitution of egos has occurred, although not in a particularly dramatic way. His predecessor in that body was dispirited and sick of politics for the sake of playing games, and was ready to depart. Since he was in a good position to step forward through name recognition, he was willing to let another take his place, and that has been effected. He is still adjusting but will be heard from more dramatically as the time approaches for the nominating conventions. He is neither liberal nor conservative, as those terms are used today. He is sensible and aware, and has great sensitivity to the needs of others. He will be nominated and elected. All for now."

The Walk-in candidate will not immediately speak of the possibility of a shift, according to the Guides, "since many are not ready for that frightening news. But he will edge into it by pointing out America's total dependency on electricity and computers, and the need to protect these sources of energy and knowledge. Some will begin to heed his words, and as election time approaches he will be a very strong contender for nomination. His levelheaded approach to problem solving will attract many to his cause."

The Guides indicate that the next president will face other domestic problems. "President Clinton's health care program will bog down in debate," they predicted, "and will not be enacted in any but minor details. Welfare reform is badly needed, since it is destroying the will of so many to earn a living, but it will also stalemate to a degree."

Skipping again to the predicted shift of the Earth, they continued: "As the time approaches, many will have stored foods and other items not dependent on electricity. They will construct shelters away from open areas, knowing that the winds will have tremendous sweep as the Earth shifts on its axis. Some will inhabit caves, such as their early ancestors did, although of course there are not enough for today's population explosion. Those who have made no preparations will have a difficult time, but they will have been duly warned.

"The weather will continue its rather freakish course, and as the time for the Shift approaches there will be tremendously damaging storms. Food will become a scarcity in wide areas of the Earth, and without the funds to send massive shipments, America will be looked upon with increasing disfavor, despite its past generosity. Medical care will dissatisfy many, as the revised system initiated by the Clintons will deplete reserves of money, and perhaps even cause shortages of medical supplies as the profit margin narrows for their production. It will be a rather bleak period for many, and the Walk-in president will have his hands full trying to appease first one group of complainers and then another. As he sees the Shift approaching he will rally the spirits of some to greater effort, particularly in the construction of habitations in the safer areas, but this will not be an easy task."

I pleaded for some cheerful news, but the Guides declared: "When the Shift approaches, there will be turmoil throughout the land. All will be turning to Washington for advice, and the new president will reassure those who wish to survive that there will be places for them in newly built shelters in what he considers to be the safest places. Those who flock there will find shelter, and ready-made occupations in preparing for more to come, plus planting seeds to survive the high-velocity winds and the storms. Since there will have been flooding in many locations, they will not settle adjacent to large rivers, but water will be available without too much effort. It will be like returning to the pioneer days in the American West, except that prior ownership by American landowners will be even less hospitable than were the Indians whose lands were seized by the white settlers. The government will have to intercede in advance, to prepare the way."

So this was the "good news" that I had requested! Perhaps they were leading up to it, because they subsequently wrote: "Newspapers and other media will have alerted all to the probability of a distinct alteration of alignment with the sun. There will be doubters, yes, but many other countries will be following the advice of the Walk-in president and preparing to evacuate their people from danger zones near coastlines.

"It may well be the most traumatic period in the history of the Earth, since modern media have never failed to warn and frighten and publicize impending disasters. For many on Earth it will be regarded as the major disaster of all times, but those who think this have forgotten that things of the spirit are far more important than those of the flesh, and that the Earth will become a cleaner, better place after the Shift."

9

THE
ANTICHRIST

Trauma, indeed! The Guides could casually speak of traumatic times ahead, but what did they think they were doing to me now? I was deeply disheartened at the thought of conveying their message to loyal readers of my books, with many of whom I had been corresponding throughout the years. It was a temptation to forget the whole project and, as the saying goes, let sleeping dogs lie.

At this despairing time, I received a copy of a college thesis written by a woman who had interviewed me many years ago concerning my close friendship with Marguerite Higgins, the Pulitzer Prize–winning journalist who covered the Korean War for the old *New York Herald-Tribune*. Marguerite had named me the godmother of her firstborn child, Larry, and when her daughter, Linda, was subsequently born, she asked Bob and me if we would take the responsibility for her children in the event that she and her husband, General William Hall, should both be killed. We naturally agreed.

A few years later Marguerite made a reportorial trip to war-torn Vietnam, but after a month she returned home with a rare tropical disease called leishmaniasis, apparently conveyed in the bite of a sand fly. She was desperately ill, and I visited her frequently at Walter Reed Hospital in Washington. One morning a mutual friend telephoned to say that Marguerite was extremely anxious to see me that very day. I was in a quandary. I was just leaving the house to appear on a television talk show, after which I had to produce my daily syndicated column, without an idea of what to write about.

I did nonetheless drive to Walter Reed, stopping en route to buy Marguerite a bright red bed jacket. She seemed cheered and immediately put it on. Then her mood changed and she asked, "Ruth, did you think I was going to die?"

Nearly everyone assumed that her disease was fatal, but I staunchly replied, "No, Marguerite, I won't let you die." After all, by then I knew that there is no such thing as death, and I fully believed that she would live on in spirit.

She smiled but added wistfully, "I wish now that I'd paid more attention to the things you're into—the psychic things—

and talked with you about them." I tried to assure her that there was plenty of time, but she looked doubtful.

During my long career as a newspaper reporter and columnist in Washington, Marguerite and I had covered many of the same events, both in the capital and abroad, but never as rivals intent on beating each other to the story. Our gardens adjoined in Georgetown, and our husbands were also friends. As her strength ebbed I offered to cancel a scheduled trip to Egypt, but neither she nor her husband would hear of it. She passed into spirit while I was away.

Recalling that sad time prompted me to ask the Guides how she was faring in the spirit plane, and they replied: "Marguerite is fully aware and says, 'Ruth, you will be glad to know that you had the best story of all to write about—what it's like on this side that is called the spirit plane [*A World Beyond*]. I am progressing and will be ready for a new try at Earth life when the opportunity presents itself. Don't get discouraged. Your writings have done so much good and will live on when our news stories are long forgotten. I appreciate your friendship.'"

Those generous words prompted me to reread a book about Marguerite called *Witness to War* that Antoinette May wrote in 1983.

I had also been interviewed for that book, and reading it again reawakened my admiration for Marguerite. As I wrote to the Guides, "She had courage, drive, and the ambition that I certainly lack now. Has she any advice for me?"

The Guides immediately produced Marguerite, who wrote: "Ruth, I was too ambitious for anybody's good. Your way was better, believe me, but don't give up now just because you don't feel well. You still have a lot to say that will help people. As I said, it's the best and most lasting story, while mine are now outdated by later events. Go to it, gal!"

Now, heartened by her encouragement, I finally decided to tackle the unpleasant subject of the Antichrist, to whom the Guides had occasionally referred. The Antichrist will be a false Messiah, hailed by people as their savior in a time of great chaos, but all the while working to generate great evil in the world. In one of my earlier books two decades ago, they reported that he was still in school and unaware of his own true identity. In 1993 they wrote that, having graduated from college sometime before, "he now holds a minor government office and is aspiring to become president. He is full of mischief but not yet fully aware of the role that he was prepared to play when he came back to this Earth life. He has his eye on the elections of 2000, when he will be barely old enough to run for the White House."

From time to time the Guides kept me posted on his "progress," if we can call it that. In May of 1994 they reported that "the Antichrist is now in a governmental position, and his name will shortly become familiar to those in the know. He is ambitious above all else, and wants power, but is only just now beginning to feel that his purpose is to be ready to seize that power when the opportunity arises." They volunteered that they see no major warfare ahead, "because although war clouds are gathering, the shift of the Earth will prevent its occurrence as people scramble to preserve their own lives rather than seek national expansionism."

Two months later they contributed another "progress report." Reminding me that the Antichrist is now in a "somewhat minor position in government," they added: "But he will begin to rise as he realizes his full potential for evil. Let us emphasize that he is not Satan, but a longtime disciple of that rebellious one, and has had many previous Earth lives. He is fairly young still, but on the borderline of becoming eligible for the presidency at the turn of the century. That will be his ambition, and after the Walk-in president is installed in office, the Antichrist will try to move forward, making waves and attracting attention.

"As the Shift approaches he will begin to propose logical-sounding propositions to solve the problems and will attract followers, as he is a compelling speaker with what will seem to be a pleasing personality. He cares nothing for truth, so he will promise everything to everyone and say that he is the one person who can lead them out of the miseries of this decade. He will not be elected in 2000, but he will move into the turmoil immediately following the Shift, calling on all to follow him, and many will do so for a time, until he is unmasked for the evil incarnate that he is."

At a later date the Guides added: "The Antichrist will make his real grab for power after the Shift, when people are beset by problems and frantic for solutions, and he will soon attempt to become a dictator with powers to regulate all human activities. This will awaken thinking people to the perils of following such a person. His true colors will be seen, and he will eventually meet physical death through violent means. We do not wish to say more about him at this time."

10

THE
AFTERMATH

Public opinion polls in recent years have listed crime as the paramount concern of Americans, and the Guides made this intriguing comment: "The violence that we are witnessing among people today is closely associated with the unparalleled turbulence and violence within the Earth itself."

Defense attorneys have lately produced such novel excuses for the actions of their clients that this might provide a new defense: "The Earth made me do it."

The Guides say that as the time grows nearer for the long-predicted Shift, the turbulence will greatly increase. "It is then that even the hard-nosed scientists will begin to accept that Earth changes are coming," they declared, "and the Walk-in president will be able to enlist their cooperation in preparing people for it. Safe havens will be readied and work made available for those who are willing to roll up their sleeves and construct facilities for the refugees who will be pouring in. There will be millions, yes, but certainly not the vast majority of the population. Many will remain unconvinced and scoff at the scare stories. Some will simply decide that the preservation of their lives is not all that important, and still others will stay behind to loot, not perhaps realizing that the things they steal will soon be useless as the Shift sweeps it all away."

The Guides gave a detailed accounting of the actual Shift in *Strangers Among Us*, predicting that it will occur "in the twinkling of an eye, as the Earth slips approximately onto its side." They said that in daylight areas the sun will seem to stand still overhead and then to race backward for a brief period while the Earth settles into its new position relative to the sun.

I now asked them to discuss the aftermath, and they pointed out that for a time there would be no electricity, "so no access to computer data, banking cards, and the like. As survivors in physical form look about them, everything will seem changed. North will not be true north, nor has it been since the last shift of the Earth millennia ago. Disorientation will occur to many, but as they begin to walk around they will find that the Earth is still solid, many trees are still in place, as are many buildings in those areas less affected by the torrential windstorms, flooding, or tidal waves.

"People will gradually begin to regroup, finding friends and new supporters, even as allied forces did after their landing at Omaha Beach on D day in World War II. Some will drop to their knees in thanksgiving for their rescue, while others will bewail the loss of homes and loved ones. But survivors they will be, and as that realization comes, so will courage and the indomitable spirit that has long been manifested in humankind. Reconstruction will begin, even as food sources are found and contact reestablished in most areas of the country. Overseas news will filter in through cabled messages, and radio will soon be operational."

The Guides said to expect turmoil for a time as water recedes from some areas and finds new channels in others. "It will take people back to the basics of living without electrical appliances, lights, cooking gases, and most fuels except wood and coal," they continued. "Some will take it with good cheer, glad to be given the opportunity to survive and start over, while others will, of course, complain; but as the evil ones die out or are dealt with for murdering to get the hoarded supplies of those who were prepared, there will be less tension and more love.

"The American pioneers were able to cope with equally drastic conditions as they first settled and then expanded to wilderness areas," they reminded me, "and some of that mighty pioneering spirit will return to a people who have grown soft, greedy, and self-centered. That will improve character, even as the survivors struggle to help one another and protect their families."

Until electricity is restored, which it will be shortly in most surviving areas, the Guides say people will need to rely on old skills such as math, rather than calculators and computers. "As for the banks, those whose money supply survives will do what they can to lend and borrow, so that currency will still be needed, but its value will be quite different. Raw materials for rebuilding will be far more valuable than cash, as will medical supplies and food."

The allusion to medical supplies prompted me to ask them a question posed by Berkley Bedell, who was instrumental in congressional passage of a two-million-dollar appropriation for a study of alternative medicine and its benefits. What do the Guides see ahead for the field of alternative medicine?

"The world after the Shift will go back to natural remedies, as were used in earlier times," they replied, "and herbs should now be grown by private citizens in preparation for that period. Doctors will again attune intuitively to the ailments of patients, relying less on X rays and chemical testing, which after all are only a hundred or so years old. Skills will be developed as people in the new age begin to look within and to harmonize themselves to universal energy, so that humans will keep in better physical condition. The modern tools of medicine are good as far as they go, but those in physical being should rely less on machines and pills and more on their inner resources."

The Guides agreed that transportation will present an immediate problem, since ships, planes, railroad tracks, and highways will be severely damaged, but they added: "Leaders in various countries will emerge with superb new ideas for dealing with the emergencies and will exchange information with the American Walk-in president."

Full of enthusiasm, they declared: "It will be an era of good feeling and good fellowship, much as in the days of the early pioneers who plunged westward to unknown territory and always found a welcome sign out for weary travelers. There will still be births among those hardy survivors, and as the vehicles become available, a loving, giving group of future leaders will inhabit those new bodies and become increasingly important as the years pass.

"The Earth will seem a splendid place, and into that era of good feeling will come the Christ, who will uplift humankind and make of the planet a model for all humanity. That is the era long spoken of as 'the Millennium,' when peace shall reign on Earth for a thousand years."

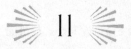

THE APOSTLES
RETURN

Wearying of hearing about the Shift, I was eager for the Guides to tell us about the age of enlightenment that they said was to follow it, but at this point a rather bizarre occurrence intervened. Within the space of a few weeks, reincarnated characters from the New Testament seemed to be dropping into my lap. The trigger for all of this apparently was my reading of a new book called *The Messengers,* written by Julia Ingram and G. W. Hardin, about Nick Bunick, a highly successful businessman from Portland, Oregon, who during thirteen hypnotic regressions seemingly relived a previous lifetime as St. Paul, recounting numerous conversations of his with Jesus in Palestine.

In *Companions Along the Way,* the Guides described a previous incarnation I am said to have had in Palestine as a sister of

Lazarus, when I had known Jesus. Under hypnosis I, too, had seemingly relived some of that lifetime. As a result, I totally agreed with every word that Paul quoted Jesus as having uttered, although I did not always agree with everything that Paul himself said. The Bible, of course, indicates that Paul never met Jesus while the latter was in physical body, but the occurrences recounted and the conversations seem so authentic that I was deeply moved by the book.

Even the circumstance of my reading the book appears to have been predestined. While I was autographing my own books after a talk given in Fort Myers, Florida, a woman named Teresa Farquhar introduced herself and said that this was the fourth time she had come to hear me speak: once in Portland, Oregon, her hometown, then in Phoenix, and twice in Fort Myers. Now she was greatly excited by a book called *The Messengers* and had brought me a copy. It is not unusual for people to give me paperback books on such occasions, but I seldom read them, because I have macular degeneration and try to save my eyesight for necessary reading.

The next day I found a letter from Teresa in the book and decided that I should at least scan it, in order to thank her for her thoughtfulness. I therefore began reading the book and could not put it down until it was finished. I wrote Teresa such an enthusiastic letter about the book that she shared it with

Nick, and he wrote to me. We kept in touch, and when he concluded a book tour, he flew to my home in Florida. With him was a friend and coworker, Brian Hilliard, and we had a wonderful visit.

I showed them a picture of a recently deceased friend of mine, Betty Arends, and remarked that the Guides had identified her as Elizabeth, mother of John the Baptist. Betty's late husband, Les Arends, of Illinois, had been the Republican leader of the House of Representatives, succeeding Jerry Ford in that position when President Nixon named the latter to be vice president of the United States. My Guides further identified Les Arends as Zacharius in that same Palestinian lifetime, the father of John the Baptist. Previously, Betty told me, three different psychics had said that she was the mother of John the Baptist. Brian Hilliard somewhat shyly remarked that several psychics had told him that he was the same soul as John the Baptist, and the next day the Guides confirmed to me that this was true.

I was surprised, as my Sunday school impression of John the Baptist was of a "wild man" who was somewhat ferocious, but Brian was a rare human being who radiated love and seemed to permeate the room with it. Later I realized that this was understandable. The Guides and Edgar Cayce have said that the Christ spirit entered Jesus of Nazareth when John baptized him, and Jesus brought forth the new commandment: Love one another.

After Betty Arends passed into spirit, she began communicating with me through the Guides, as my late husband, Bob, has also done. She described a gloriously happy reunion with her husband, Les, and when I asked her if she had seen her son, John the Baptist, she replied that he had reincarnated. After Brian was here, the Guides said Betty was ecstatic to see John at my house from her spirit plane.

On the memorable day that the reincarnated souls of St. Paul and John the Baptist spent at my penthouse overlooking the Gulf of Mexico, I invited a close friend, Leize Perlmutter, to join us, because the Guides had said that she knew me in the Palestinian lifetime. They now declared that Leize had lived in Hebron then and was the daughter of Joseph of Arimathea, who according to the Bible claimed the body of Jesus from the cross and provided his own unused tomb as the burial place for Christ. The famous medium Arthur Ford was then my father, a Jewish rabbi named Jeremiah, and we lived nearby in Bethany, according to the Guides. Joseph was a member of the Sanhedrin, the supreme council of the Jews, and an admirer of Jesus, and he always spoke out in his defense. Leize's name was then said to be Sarah, and our two families were devoted friends. They said my name was Ruth, the eldest sister of Lazarus, Martha, and Mary, also identified as such in the classic book *The Aquarian Gospel of Jesus the Christ.* This is said to be from the Akashic records transcribed by Levi H. Dowling (1844–1911), a Disciples of Christ minister and physician.

Previously the Guides had told me that when Mary and Joseph took Jesus to Egypt, to escape Herod's edict that all baby boys in Palestine under the age of two were to be killed, Arthur Ford (Jeremiah) took our family with them, because Lazarus was the same age as Jesus, and Joseph was our kinsman. We spent the next several years together in Egypt, where Lazarus and Jesus were inseparable playmates, and all of us adored Jesus for his uncommon wisdom and charm.

Previously the Guides had told me that my husband, Bob Montgomery, had been my husband, Jonathan, in the Palestinian incarnation, and our two daughters then were now my sister, Margaret Forry, of Indianapolis, and a good friend, Rachel Carr, who is a talented artist and book author, now living in a Maryland suburb of Washington, D.C.

Leize had already read *The Messengers* and was as moved by it as I was. Thus it was a happy reunion for all of us, as if two thousand years had not elapsed since we last met. The four of us kept in close touch thereafter, by telephone and E-mail, and when I learned that Nick and Brian had a friend who had been told that he was St. Peter, I asked the Guides about him. They replied that Peter was not now incarnated, and that the friend had actually been a friend of Paul's who sometimes traveled with him in those Palestinian days.

Now I became curious about my alleged onetime brother, Lazarus, about whose life the Guides had gone into such detail in *Companions Along the Way*. Is he now incarnated, and do I know him? I was aware that Edgar Cayce, America's most famous seer, had during his lifetime identified two women as Martha and Mary, but where was Lazarus?

The Guides obligingly wrote that I know him very well now as Joe Spano. Aha! My own cherished physician, who is a highly respected gastroenterologist in Naples, Florida, and who regularly conducts a meditation group at Unity Church. The next time I saw Joe after delivering this message, he said that he often senses Jesus beside him saying, "No, you don't want to do that," or "Try it this way instead."

My friend Leize is quite psychic, and one day she said her intuition had been telling her that her husband had been St. Luke, "the dear and glorious physician." The Guides agreed that Dr. David Perlmutter, a neurologist who now practices alternative medicine in Naples, was indeed Luke, and "in this lifetime he is subconsciously recalling his association with Jesus, Paul, and the other disciples, to the great advantage of his practice and his work, as he realizes that he is an innate healer who can go far deeper than the medical way in healing patients. He is a good, good soul."

The Guides further said that Joseph of Arimathea still loves Leize very much, watches over her, and influenced her to marry David, as well as influenced their two children to select Leize and David as their parents in this lifetime. This prompted me to ask if the two children were also in that Palestinian life, and they wrote that little Reisha was then a sister of Leize's. Both girls knew Jesus then and often traveled with their father, Joseph, on his ships around the Mediterranean Sea, and even to Glastonbury in England. Leize's son, Austin, lived nearby in Hebron, and although not related was "closer than kin." Austin adored David (Luke), who was too old to be a playmate, as he was a mature man when the others were growing up, and they held him in great esteem. Austin's name then was David and Reisha was Anna. They added that we all knew one another.

Subsequently the Guides declared that Austin's mother in the Palestinian lifetime is now his grandmother, Joyce Lamb, a cherished friend of mine who is the mother of Leize Perlmutter. They added that in Palestine "all of you loved her," meaning Joyce, and that "she was a good influence on all of you and was devoted to Jesus. Far and wide she spread His message."

At this point I received a bundle of fan letters forwarded by my publishers, and one of them was from a man who said he had been told twenty years ago by a psychic that he was Nicodemus and that his own memories told him this was true. The timing was intriguing, so I asked the Guides if this was correct and if they had prompted his communication. They admitted to both and said they had tried to send him a message to write me. The man is John Hitch, of Oxford, Michigan, who wrote, "In my early twenties I went to see a movie called *The Robe,* with Victor Mature. I was in great expectation to see the robe all the way through. When they finally did show the robe, everything in me cried out, '*No, no.* It's not right. It's not even the right color or shape.' I left the movie after it ended feeling very let down. Many years later, while reading *Edgar Cayce's Story of Jesus,* by Jeffrey Furst, I learned of a reading given by Cayce for a woman who had been the wife of Nicodemus in that life and it was she who had woven the wonderful robe on her own loom. The color was described as silver-white and made from lamb's wool, and my inner self said that at last they had it right as I remembered it.

"After I received a copy of *The Aquarian Gospel of Jesus the Christ,* I learned much more about my life as Nicodemus: how he tried valiantly to defend Jesus during his trial at the Sanhedrin, but to no avail. After the crucifixion he worked with Joseph of Arimathea to secure permission from Pilate to take the body of Jesus to its burial. Now what I want to do is correct some of the errors in the Gospels. First, Pontius Pilate was not a bad guy. He tried very hard to save the life of Jesus. He told Jesus that he would give him a horse and a group of soldiers for escort, to get him out of Jerusalem to safety. Jesus of course said he could not go. Pilate did not scourge Jesus. There were five Roman soldiers assigned to King Herod, and these were the ones who scourged him, mocked him, and gave him his crown of thorns.

"Okay, one more. Why was Jesus unable to carry his cross? When Jesus was condemned to death by the Sanhedrin, under Jewish law he could be stoned to death, and nothing more. The mob, led by the high priest, took Jesus to the gates of the city, and they began to stone him. At this time, three of the Roman soldiers who were Herod's guard came by, and the high priest pleaded with them to crucify Jesus, since that was a Roman way of execution. Because Jesus was already half dead and could barely walk, he could not carry a cross, too. These soldiers were quick to oblige, and of course the rest is history."

I asked the Guides why all of us Palestinians had come back at this particular time, and they replied: "Because it is the dawn of a new millennium, which means a new start; a clean slate, so to speak. All of you wanted to be present for the changes that will occur in the new era of enlightenment and to help guide it along, as all of you are doing. It is akin to a spiritual cleansing of humankind, and you who had been present at the time of Jesus' sojourn in Earthly embodiment wish again to avail yourselves of the spiritual cleansing, and to help others find it. It is more than coincidence that so many of you have found one another. Nick's book certainly played a role, as did each of you, in being open to this exciting time."

Still amazed by the wonder of it all, I asked why they all seemed to be getting in touch with me. They wrote: "Because your own self has deepened in spirituality, and you are subconsciously putting out waves of welcome and understanding. You are supposed to write a book about this regathering of the Palestinians. That is why we have brought you all this material."

With their acknowledgment that *The Messengers* had been a catalyst, I asked if Teresa Farquhar, the fan who brought the book to me, had been with us in that Palestinian life, and they wrote, "Yes, yes, yes! We arranged for her to bring you that book. She was one of us [Arthur Ford was speaking] in that lifetime, and a remarkable soul who understood God's teachings from the very beginning. Of course you all knew Saul [Paul]. Teresa was a live wire who also spread the good news. You were drawn together in this lifetime, as all the good shepherds are, in these latter days before the dawn of the new age, and you all feel a bonding to one another."

12

OTHER PALESTINIANS

Dan Haley of Dallas, a onetime New York legislator, seems always to be doing thoughtful things for others. I therefore asked the Guides whether he had been known to me in the Palestinian life, and as I asked the question, the word *Timothy* flashed through my mind. The name meant nothing to me, but the Guides calmly wrote: "Yes, he was Timothy, as you sensed. In that lifetime he was as intense about spreading the word of the Lord as he is this time around about alternative medicine. He has always been intent on helping others, and doing whatever he can to further the cause. You and Bob [my then-husband, Jonathan] knew him well in your travels around the region, where you were carrying the message of Jesus, and all of you knew Paul then."

But who was Timothy? A Microsoft encyclopedia identified him as "Saint Timothy, a Christian missionary: intimate friend and trusted disciple of Saint Paul." It said that he was born in the ancient district of Lycania in Turkey, the son of a Gentile father and Jewish mother. "As assistant to Paul, Timothy was entrusted with several important missions to churches that Paul had founded. After Paul's release from prison in Rome, he joined Timothy in the East and later left him in charge at Ephesus, a position of great responsibility." There was much more about Timothy.

Through Dan, I met Don Rott, a Dallas businessman and utopian planner, who after several meetings somewhat reluctantly told me that his own Guide, Amatamaji, had identified him as the reborn soul of the youngest disciple, John. My Guides, on being queried, replied: "Yes, he was. He was very gifted and still tries to help people, as did St. John. He knew Timothy in that lifetime, which explains their friendship now. You knew them both in Palestine."

Don said he felt sure that a present-day doctor friend was his brother James in Palestine, and the Guides confirmed it. But they denied Don's further hunch that one of his current best friends was Judas. I was relieved, since I would not want to brand any living person as the traitorous Judas.

It seemed of interest, however, that now the disciple James, along with St. Luke and Lazarus, had all returned in this lifetime as medical doctors. Could it be due to their subconscious memory of Jesus' healing ministry?

The Guides did not confine themselves to biblical characters. Many of my current friends were identified as friends from the Palestinian lifetime. Ninette Peterson, an astrologer and ordained minister who founded the Aquarian Center in Naples, was then named Hannah, "a good neighbor indeed in Bethany, who was like a mother to the whole small community. Everyone turned to her for solace and encouragement. She knew Jesus, of course, and Lazarus very well; and Arthur Ford, who was then your father, knew her and loved her, too. Mary was your youngest sister, as we have told you, and is now on this side of the veil. Edgar Cayce correctly identified her and Martha many years ago."

Another time I asked the Guides if I had known Betty Mills, a close friend in Naples, in any previous lifetime, and they wrote, "We've been looking into it and find that it ties into the Palestinian life, when she lived near to you in Bethany. Her family and yours were close friends, and when you returned from Egypt they were still there, although they had lost one member of the family, not a firstborn son, but another who died of an illness. You sympathized deeply with Betty, whose name then was also Elizabeth, and she knew Mary and Martha, too, although she was older than them, as were you."

In my earlier books the Guides had said that good friends and relatives in previous lifetimes tend to reincarnate together, into circumstances where they will find one another. I therefore asked if my closest friend for the past half century, Hope Ridings Miller, of Washington, D.C., had been in the Palestinian life, and what about Polly Claxton of Gainesville, Texas, who designs lovely costume jewelry and generously shares it with others?

The Guides wrote: "Yes, you knew them both. Hope was your favorite cousin, and she lived in Bethany near you. Her father was a brother of Arthur Ford's [Jeremiah], and they were devoted to each other. You and Hope always preferred each other's company as playmates, and her name then was Anna. The present Polly lived in Hebron and also knew you through relatives there. She was then Miriam, and she was very creative in the artistic fields. That period molded all of you for the ages to come and holds a deep meaning for you now. One could not encounter the Savior and not be instantly changed forever, so powerful was His message and His personality."

Seemingly out of the blue I received a telephone call from Marianne Williamson, the popular author and lecturer in the spiritual field, and because of the timing I asked the Guides if I had known her in the Palestinian lifetime. They replied in the affirmative, writing: "She is a highly developed soul who will leave a lasting impression for good in this world, as she will inspire so many others. She is high-minded and a born leader who knew you then, when she was also one of the followers of Jesus. She lived in Bethany when you did and knew Lazarus and many of the disciples. An outstanding woman then, as now."

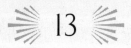

13

LAZARUS LIVES AGAIN

For anyone who fears the Shift and is afraid of death, perhaps the most reassuring part of the New Testament is the story of Lazarus, who is said to have died and been sealed in a tomb for three days before Jesus called him back to life. It is also one of the greatest mysteries of the Bible. Where was Lazarus during that interim? When word reached me that Julia Ingram, the noted therapist from Oregon who had hypnotically regressed Nick Bunick to his seeming lifetime as St. Paul, was coming to Naples, I suggested that Dr. Joseph Spano submit to hypnosis to see if he could tap into his alleged life as Lazarus. Joe agreed, and as the adventure began he described himself as a lad of thirteen, wearing somewhat ragged trousers, a homespun shirt, and sandals, hiking along a stream under willow trees.

Asked by Julia if he was alone, he replied that in the distance he could see his family reunion in progress—a number of close-knit families were participating in a discussion (by the men) of what the future of the youngsters should be: whether they would be sent off to school or kept at home. Under questioning, Lazarus said his own preference would be to stay at home and do farm chores.

"I love the Earth," he explained. "I love walking upon the ground and feeling earth, and seeing the beauty of the surroundings."

Asked where he lived, he described a small village near Jerusalem that he identified as Bethany, populated by "probably fifteen families." Asked what was occurring, he replied: "Well, the men talk sometimes very heatedly and forcefully, but not in a hostile manner. One can feel free to state differences of opinion. They are talking about what should be the future of the older children: who should be chosen to go where, based upon what aptitudes they have shown. There is a strong separation here between women and men. The men are creating almost an illusion that they are in control, but the women can gently make their own desires known and can influence the men."

In answer to Julia's questions, Joe (as Lazarus) spoke of his sisters, saying: "Martha is a very forthright person who speaks her mind and is very businesslike. There is no ambiguity here; she is very certain. You know where Martha stands on things. She doesn't lord it over me, but always teaches me something. She is taking the place of our deceased mother. She has a lot of chores to do, but she accepts this as though it is something she is not 'resigned to' but likes to do. With Mary I can see the wheels always going. She is thinking, thinking and absorbing. She is very quiet, almost at times withdrawn. A dear, sweet person."

Julia asked about his eldest sister, Ruth, and Lazarus indicated that he didn't know her very well, as she was no longer living at home. (I was probably married to Jonathan and living in Jericho by then.) "Father is a rabbi. He has very definite ideas of what women should be like, and although Ruth was very smart, very bright, quite intelligent, she desired to explore things that Father disapproved of. They were mysterious things. I hear that she is very well versed in the ancient mysteries. One might call her somewhat of a priestess. It is something to do with temples of Egypt, maybe something with Isis. Some of the women still have an affinity for that material, our ancestors having lived in Egypt for so long. There is no group who lives in any distant country that doesn't take on some of the attributes of that society, and this mystery is something that is common to Egypt and our people. It was an ancient teaching, something Ruth would have had in common with Jesus. She may even have taught Him."

Julia urged Joe to recall the last time that he had seen his friend Jesus, and he said, "He is part of the reunion. We love to walk here in this area and feel the dirt under our feet and wade in the stream. We do things like throwing rocks, seeing them skip on the water. He is a wonderful person. There is something that sets Him apart; you can feel it, but He is extremely warm, and no matter who you are, He is a dear friend, someone you know you can count on. And I enjoy Him so much because we have in common the love of the Earth. He gets so much joy out of just seeing the sights. He beats me soundly in running races."

Asked if Jesus' future was also being discussed by the men at the reunion, Joe (Lazarus) replied, "Yes, He has exhibited what they say is wisdom beyond His years, and so the decision is whether He is going to a 'special' school. There is one near here, you know. It is always talked about in reverent terms— hush, hush. Our family knows it well. Others outside of the family sometimes make remarks about it that are not so nice: 'peculiar people and weird.' It is an Essene school. To go there is a big commitment, and you won't see your family much, plus it's hard, intensive study. I know already it is not for me. I like just what I am doing now, but Jesus wants to go. He already has knowledge that He needs to go there, and I can see when talking with Him about His future, that it is one of great importance.

"The families say Jesus is like a chosen one, but His faith has taken off in directions that they don't fully agree with: that our present faith is overregulated, too many man-made rules. It has become too secular, and is not abiding by the basic fundamental precepts of all our ancestors. Jesus says we need to return to some of those basic ways of worship of God and the Earth, because we are fundamentally Earth-bound people. Too much ritual has been entrenched in the synagogues. They are getting away from direct contact with the people who are out in the villages. We in the villages are very happy people with just the basic life, with our homes and animals."

Julia moved Joe forward six years, to the age of nineteen, and asked if he still sees Jesus. He responded: "When He leaves the Essene community we sometimes meet here in Bethany. Our warmth and love for each other are very deep, but I can see that he has grown by leaps and bounds beyond me. So we mainly reminisce and recall what we did, but we have learned many things together."

Asked if Jesus had stayed mainly at the school, he said, "Well, He has told me that He has gone back to Egypt, and while there engrossed Himself in the ancient wisdom, but from what He tells me, it is just a refresher course. Many of these things He sensed that He already knew. It is all part of one information, just a different way of presenting its different trappings, different tools and sacred objects."

Lazarus described his close friend as handsome, lean, and muscular, continuing: "It is so hard to describe Jesus. No matter who you are, you can relate to Him. There is some way that you can connect to Him, and He just radiates the something that sets Him apart, yet connects Him right to your own essence. It is like He can meet a person and go into their energy to meet them. You can be the most muscular, macho-type man, you can be one of the wrestlers or gladiators. Even the Roman soldiers appreciate that this is a special man. They can feel the strength, the health and vitality in Him. The word is like 'honor this person.'"

Lazarus said his father had passed on, and he himself was still living the life that he enjoyed, taking care of the home and his two sisters. He was also calling on the young ladies of the vicinity. Two years later in that lifetime, Lazarus reported that it was a very difficult time for him, because he was in love with a girl named Leath and he was "torn." Asked why that was difficult, he said he had promised his father to take care of his sisters, but his sisters wanted him "to marry into a higher-up family, that is more of our rank, the lineage of David. Leath's family are more simple folk, and to me that is somewhat appealing. They are very genuine, but still there is pressure to marry within your own level," so he gave up his sweetheart, admitting that he himself wasn't too keen on surrendering his own freedom.

Julia wanted to know why his two sisters still living at home had not married, and Lazarus reported: "With Martha, I think her bossiness turned off a lot of suitors, and Mary has had men call upon her, but she is my little sister and I have not given my approval yet." Asked how he supported his family, he said, "We have some farmland that brings some income, and we raise animals, and Father left us some money. Our needs are not great. We have no aspirations to travel far and wide, so we are comfortable and our needs are met."

Julia moved him forward to age thirty-one and asked what Jesus was then doing. Lazarus responded that "He has begun teaching, and is beginning to make a name for Himself."

Julia: "What are people saying?"

Lazarus: "Some are just confused; they are not sure who He is. Others are very much enthralled by the message He brings, and some are disturbed. Those who are dedicated to protecting the present Jewish laws are very visibly disturbed. They want the status quo and are saying things that could easily inflame, but that's from their own perspective. What I hear

Him say is always beautiful and very inspiring. It is controversial, but the people out in the villages accept this much more readily than those in the larger cities. So many of us have had lives of desperation that are apart from the experiences of those who are in higher positions in the faith, so to us His words have meaning, because we are so much more attuned to the Earth. His is a simple, eloquent message of wisdom."

Lazarus said that he occasionally went to the Essene community when there were visiting speakers. One particularly impressed him, a Chinese astrologer who brought information about the wisdom of the stars, and "it dovetailed with all of the information brought by other scholars, including Tibetans." Julia asked if he had any theories on how the same information could be so widely dispersed, and Lazarus said, "I think there must be angels or guides who can communicate with us, if we just listen. This is what the scholars say: If we go into a deep introspection, information can come, so that must be how it works. You just tap into it. There are teachers on other planes that are teaching, and who are listening, anyway."

Julia then directed the conversation to the time that Lazarus became very ill and reportedly died, and asked if the reports were true.

Lazarus: "Yes, I had become very ill, and there were fevers and rigors. I couldn't eat. There were pains and sweating,

sweating, sweating. I became weaker and weaker. I am very thin, and my sisters are wiping me down with cool linens, trying to keep the fever down, and they have tried all their herbal remedies, but I continue to be ill, and they are frantic. But there is something very strange. Jesus is telling me not to worry."

Julia: "He is there?"

Lazarus: "He is not there in the physical. He is reassuring me that He would never abandon me, so I have no fear. I've an incredible sense of being nurtured. I feel a darkness descend and I have no awareness."

Julia: "What is happening to the body now? What is happening to the spirit?"

Lazarus: "My spirit is separating and merging with something independent, yet with something larger, and the body is very gray, very still, so I can see the body."

Julia: "Can you see the silver cord? What happens next?"

Lazarus: "The cord is like a tongue of light, just a tiny thread. The sisters are crying and wailing. They don't want to believe that I am dead. Martha is upset because she thought Jesus would intervene, but as I see it now, I can understand at a much deeper level that it was very important for Him to wait for me to die. This was very crucial in His going on to be glorified."

Julia: "So you have agreed to this?"

Lazarus: "Yes, in our deeper communication it was an agreement, from the beginning of time. Friends and family confirm that I am dead."

Julia: "How much time passes before He actually arrives?"

Lazarus: "Well, I am already removed to the tomb, and this must be the fourth day. I had been treated with the precious oils, wrapped in linens, and carried to the tomb, which was then sealed. I wish I could have told them not to worry, but this all seemed to be part of a larger plan, and in the three days there was just darkness. There was like a descent process. It is as if you go to the center of the Earth. At that point, all is revealed and any impurities have been cleansed."

Asked what was revealed to him, he replied enigmatically, "I cannot say." Julia then moved him forward to Jesus' arrival, and Lazarus continued: "I was in the midst of having just come out of the darkness, moving into light, and at the moment that the light struck me, I felt like it distracted me. It was as though someone in a dark room turned on a light, and I heard His voice. I already had full knowledge that I would go back. There was, of course, some reluctance, but this was extraordinary: now placed out of the darkness into the light. It would have been nice to stay, but I knew I must go back."

Julia: "So you heard His voice?"

Lazarus: "Yes, I heard His voice. The tomb was opened and he came in. A streak of light again, and He is all light, and He extends His light to my body, and it is hard to describe how I knew I was going into the body, and He was extending life force into the body."

Julia: "I understand. There is a lot of light in this room around you right now. It is an incredible light."

Lazarus: "It is as though there is a merging of Him and me together, and suddenly I am physical; and as I go out of the tomb we have the linens to take off. I am shocked again at my body. I am just a shell of what I was, but I am alive. I have had the most thorough cleansing! It was very important that this happened. It was very, very crucial, because the people saw Him bring me back. They had seen Him make the lame walk, and cleanse the leper, but in a day or two they forgot. What really would impress is if someone is raised from death, and thus it is very important. I think Isaiah did it, one of our wonderful ancestors, but that was a miracle of miracles. Now the word just spreads like wildfire, and I am a reluctant celebrity. I would like just to return to how I was before, but people want to touch me. They feel as though I have taken on some sort of holy nature. I have to remind them that it was the Christ who did it."

Julia: "There is more light in your body now. I can see it."

Lazarus: "Yes, I feel very different. I feel that whereas there may have been some skepticism or doubt, now I am very sure of all that Jesus has represented. There is no doubt at all. I am satisfied that I must show people that I do live, to verify that Jesus is the Christ. But now people are telling me that the Pharisees want to see me dead, because they realize the importance of Christ raising someone up from the dead, and they would like to have me dead again right away, to extinguish that."

Asked what he did about the threat to his life, Lazarus said he tried to see only those who were "with us," and he agreed with them that he should not go to Jerusalem, because "they are waiting for me" there. "It is certainly true that Jesus now has the die cast, that He must go on to His destiny and death, because now the Pharisees are really talking death to Him. They want to be rid of Jesus. This episode sets the stage for His death and resurrection. He is now gathering followers by the hundreds and hundreds, and this worries the synagogue because of the old Herod stuff that was still floating around, the old 'King of the Jews' rumors. In order to maintain the status quo he had to go, and this was the final straw."

Julia: "How long did it take you to recover your strength and gain your weight back?"

Lazarus: "It was very slow, and actually I never did return to good health. The spirit was strong, but the body was not the same, and I aged very quickly, but I understood I had already accomplished what I needed to do."

Asked what happened next, he replied: "Well, Jesus comes back to our home in Bethany and it is a wonderful reunion. We have a meal prepared for Him and His closest disciples. It was close to Passover, when everyone goes to Jerusalem, but His advisors are saying this is a year for Him not to go; but He already knows that He must go. This is part of the drama that has to be enacted."

Julia asked if Lazarus was acquainted with Joseph of Arimathea, and he replied: "Yes, he is a wonderful man who has been very successful in his business, and he has provided funds for many people, including Jesus. He has offered to give us money, too, but we are fine. We have no great needs. Joseph was one of those who came to advise Jesus not to go to Jerusalem, but you could see the handwriting on the wall. He had to go for Passover, because He was now being called the 'Great Rabbi,' and not to go would actually have negated a lot of what He has already accomplished."

Julia next suggested that Lazarus spare himself the painful recall of Jesus' death and instead skip to the Resurrection.

Lazarus: "Right. The Crucifixion is the most horrible thing that anyone could experience, to watch someone so loved and dear to you have that happen to him. I can only assure you that it did happen, and after the interment, He too made the descent. I don't understand why no one is exempt from the so-called descent until the third day. It is as though you have to go and pay homage to all of those who have died, and it is a connection that is indescribable. But there is some necessity, and in a way you feel more enriched. It is almost a feeling of ancestral material, too."

Asked if he saw Jesus again after His death, he replied: "I know some did and some didn't. I did not actually see Him again until after I had passed on. But I had this overwhelming sense of His being around, and not being visible, but present, and all of the family did as well. It was as though you could almost touch Him. You ask how long I lived after His crucifixion. I have a sense of four or five years."

Julia wanted to know what his life was like after the Resurrection of Jesus, and Lazarus said, "No longer did I have to be so concerned about those people who just wanted to see me, because a much greater story had now taken place—His resurrection. My purpose was again to see the people who were traveling to the Dead Sea Essene community and to visit the sacred places and Jerusalem. It was a rather quiet life after that. It was not quiet for the disciples and the apostles; they were busy, but my life became again very quiet."

Instructed to move forward to his second death in that

lifetime, Lazarus said, "This was a very easy, fast death. There was just a short illness, like a grippe, and I went very quickly. I was quite ready for death, and it was not painful, just very gentle and easy."

Urged to recount what happened after this second death, he responded: "It was just pulsating light. It was just love. That is all I feel."

After bringing him out of his altered state of consciousness, Julia said to Dr. Spano: "Welcome back. I can't tell you how bright the room became and then you got so bright. I could see it and feel it. That was amazing: to feel the light and the way it brings the light into you. That was fascinating!"

I was not present during Joe Spano's hypnotic session, but the transcript of it puzzled me. The recounting of his death and return as Lazarus did not sound at all like the occurrences described by so many of those who have had near-death experiences and relate that after the tunnel episode they had joyous reunions with loved ones. The nearest approximation was contained in the Apostles' Creed, which says of Jesus' death: "He descended into Hell. The third day He arose again from the dead."

I asked the Guides for an explanation, and they replied that although they had not personally experienced the descent, Joe in his altered state of consciousness while hypnotized was probably able to recall vividly the physical happenings in his lifetime as Lazarus but perhaps was unable to enter into the metaphysical state of death in that long-ago lifetime. He therefore could not tap into memories of the momentous event.

Still later, patiently responding to more prodding questions, the Guides wrote: "We are unfamiliar with the three-day descent and did not experience it ourselves, as far as we know. Lazarus may have been experiencing the subsequent time that Jesus spent in the tomb before rising. The purpose of restoring life to Lazarus was to demonstrate that there is no death. We are alive whether in physical body or not. Therefore, none should fear the Shift. The good part of it will be the way it changes the attitudes of those still in flesh, who will go through a personal metamorphosis as the old hatreds die out. Minds will be cleared and all will understand that as survivors they are brothers and sisters—all of one flesh."

Therefore, why dread the Shift? The Earth will quickly stabilize, and the participants will have experienced an exciting adventure. Those who pass into spirit will have front-row seats at the greatest show on Earth.

14

THE MILLENNIUM

Lily and the group had long promised that our patience and curiosity to know about the millennium would be rewarded if we would first permit them to walk us through the next few years before, during, and after the shift of the Earth on its axis.

The time had now arrived, and before launching their discussion of the good news, they had an admonition for us all. "As we approach the dawn of the millennium, let us take stock," they began. "Have you accomplished your goals? Has the world profited by your return to physical being in this present incarnation? Are others helped by your presence or harmed by your selfish ambitions? If you cannot return to physical being for another thousand years, due to the scarcity of available vehicles [babies' bodies], will you review your sins of omission and commission and yearn to do a far better job the next time around, or will you fritter away the intervening spirit phase as well?

"This is stock-taking time for all of you in physical body. Try to think of this as you fall asleep at night and as you awaken in the morning. Strive to make each day a little better because you are there to help. Bless the Earth with all your being and also those with whom you come in contact. Strive for perfection in these remaining days before the Earth so drastically changes."

Rereading this admonition brought to mind the message that my father conveyed to me from the spirit plane long ago, in *A Search for the Truth*. Cautioning that when we pass into spirit we will have to "assess the entire pages of our life," he counseled: "How much easier the task will be to review your past life, if you live each day as if that was the sole recording of your entire lifetime. Keep that page so neat and tidy, so filled with loving care, that if your life ended at midnight the page would be spotless and blameless, for surely even the worst of us can live one day in nearly blameless harmony with all about us."

Dad said we should therefore set our goal for perfect living no further than one day ahead, then set a similar goal for the next day and then the next. I particularly like to recall his

THE WORLD TO COME

summation: "Thus, you will soon have a string of pearls, each more glistening and pure than the one before, because as we live in this way, so do we grow in beauty and perfection."

Since receiving that loving counsel, I have tried to visualize each day as a flawless pearl, but somehow my own pearls develop flaws. I comfort myself by recalling those marvelous lines from Robert Browning's "Andrea del Sarto," "Ah, but a man's reach should exceed his grasp, or what's a heaven for?"

The Guides now began their discussion of the twenty-first century by writing: "Shortly after the Antichrist is put to death, the one who will become the Christ will be born into physical being. Again He will come as a babe, but because the Earth will be so changed geographically at that time, we are unable to say where His birth will occur. He is an already perfected soul who would not need to return to Schoolhouse Earth, but will volunteer to do so in order to usher in the millennium and advance the spiritual grace of all humankind."

Stressing that He will not be Jesus, "but another perfected soul," they continued: "This time He will be recognized by many as the recipient of the Christ spirit, which may enter Him in late childhood, and His goodness will be apparent to all. Remember that the times will be different then, and most of the evil ones will already have perished in Earthly form. Goodness will prevail, and those who then inhabit the Earth will have earned the right to sustain their bodies or to return there from the space sojourn that we have described.

"Ruth, we are telling you truth, not fiction. This is why no one should fear the coming Shift. It is but a pimple on the sands of time. That stirring event will open human minds as never before to the potential for the conquering of all space; not just the galaxy in which they live, but all space and all time. Yes, they will be able to move back and forth in time with as much ease as they now do in space. It is a marvelous time ahead, so be of good cheer, all of you Earthlings, for it is all in God's plan and will come to pass much sooner than anyone in Earthly body can now conceive."

I asked the Guides if it is extraterrestrials who will teach us mental space travel, and they replied in the negative, explaining, "It is the enlightened beings who will be coming into human bodies after the Shift who will bring in that knowledge. Just as the returned apostles and Palestinians are reminding Earthlings now of the spiritual laws they learned at the feet of Jesus the Christ, so the new entries will bring in advanced knowledge. The Lemurians now beginning to return, who will soon be a deluge, are so much more knowledgeable about spiritual matters and the potentials of humans than the fading-out Atlanteans have been. They will know better how to care for their bodies and minds, and to teach it to those already in physical being."

What more was there to say? I asked the Guides if they cared to summarize these extraordinary prognostications that were so difficult to digest, and they wrote: "The Christ who will enter the body of a perfected soul in the next century is the segment of God that has entered only a few chosen mortals, making them holy. During the coming golden age, while He reigns through love, peace will prevail on Earth, and all will live in harmony. As we see it from here, a selective process will be utilized to ensure that only those of goodwill are to be permitted access to the bodies of new babes, so that all evil ones will be prohibited from Earthly abode.

"As we have previously noted, men's minds will be opened to mental communication with those at a distance, and to many in the spirit plane. Space travel by mental process, as we have described, will obviate the necessity for lunar and other space vessels, just as mental communication will antiquate the telephone systems of today."

Perhaps I registered a flicker of doubt, because they wrote: "This sounds fanciful to Earthlings, as we are aware, but a couple of hundred years ago who could then have visualized today's airplanes, automobiles, spaceships, television, radio, or even electric lights? As we said, the Earth is speeding up in its development, and just as you may smile today at the Pony Express, so will succeeding generations smile at today's mechanical conveyances."

And what lies beyond the beyond? The Guides concluded their dissertation this way: "Beyond the thousand years of peace we cannot see, for it has not yet been unfolded. But this we do know—planet Earth is now about to enter its golden age, and it will be just as exciting to watch from the spirit plane as it will be for those fortunate ones who will be walking on the Earth during the reign of the Christ."

The curtain drops, but the play goes on. Other acts will follow, so don't go away. Perhaps we can meet here again in another thousand years, to unravel the continuing plot that leads to the denouement—life everlasting! Until then, *adiós* but not good-bye.

NOTE

After publication of my two books on Walk-ins, some of my Walk-in readers formed an international organization called WE (Walk-ins for Evolution). It can be contacted by writing to Liz Nelson, founder-president, at WE International, P.O. Box 120633, St. Paul, MN 55112. It publishes a monthly newsletter for and from Walk-ins, recounting their experiences, and holds regular seminars throughout the country and abroad.

Readers can write to me through my publishers. All letters are read and enjoyed, but for lack of time I cannot ask the Guides your personal questions, and can only respond to those letters that enclose self-addressed, stamped envelopes.

RUTH MONTGOMERY

INDEX

INDEX